You Are
Not Alone

You Are Not Alone

A Guide for Battered Women

Third Edition

Linda P. Rouse

ISBN 1-55691-182-3

Learning Publications, Inc.
5351 Gulf Drive
P.O. Box 1338
Holmes Beach, FL 34218-1338

Printing: 5 4 3 2 1   Year: 4 3 2 1 0

Cover design by Vicki DiOrazio and Tomara Kafka

Printed in the United States of America.

Contents

Acknowledgments

To all persons involved in making this book possible, my sincere thanks:

- To Margo Bidleman and Dr. Barbara Mills at the YWCA Domestic Assault Program in Kalamazoo, Michigan, for their interest and guidance.

- To Maureen Kilkelly at the Kalamazoo YWCA, Bob Pangle at the Prosecuting Attorney's Office, and Officer Steven Kelly of the Marshall Police Department for taking time out to talk about the legal system.

- To Professor Trudy Mills, Department of Sociology, University of Arizona for permission to use illustrative case material from her paper, "Understanding Victims of Wife Abuse: Five Stages."

- To Pamela Hayman for sharing her case notes, her wisdom, and her enthusiasm.

- To Edward Gondolf and Lou Okun for sharing their insights from counseling battering men.

- To Danna Downing and Edsel Erickson for their commitment to this book, their editing skills, and their personal support.

Finally, to women who have been battered, an acknowledgment of the courage with which they struggle to survive, physically and emotionally. I hope that this book will help make a difference in their lives.

Persons Raped or Physically Assaulted by an Intimate Partner in Lifetime and in Previous 12 Months by Sex of Victim

In Lifetime[a]

Type of Violence	Percentage Women (n=8,000)	Percentage Men (n=8,000)	Number[b] Women (100,697,000)	Number[b] Men (92,748,000)
Rape[c]	7.7	0.3	7,753,669	278,244
Physical assault[c]	22.1	7.4	22,254,037	6,863,352
Rape and/or physical assault[c]	24.8	7.6	24,972,856	7,048,848

In Previous 12 Months[a]

Type of Violence	Percentage Women (n=8,000)	Percentage Men (n=8,000)	Number[b] Women (100,697,000)	Number[b] Men (92,748,000)
Rape[c]	0.2	—[e]	201,394	—[e]
Physical assault[c]	1.3	0.9	1,309,061	834,732
Rape and/or physical assault[c]	1.5	0.9	1,510,455	834,732

[a]Intimate partner includes current and former spouses, opposite-sex cohabiting partners, same-sex cohabiting partners, dates, and boyfriends/girlfriends.
[b]Based on estimates of men and women in the United States aged 18 years or older, U.S. Bureau of the Census, Current Population Survey, 1995.
[c]Differences between women and men are statistically significant: p-value < .001.
[d]Differences between women and men are statistically significant: p-value < .05.
[e]The number of men rape victims was insufficient to reliably calculate prevalence estimates.

Source: *Research in Brief.* National Institute of Justice, U.S. Department of Justice, November 1998.

1
Are You a Battered Woman?

The term "battered woman" is used to describe women who have been the target of abusive behavior by a man who is not a stranger to them. Abusive behavior takes many forms.

Physical Abuse

The type of abuse most often associated with the term battered woman is direct physical attack. This is also called "domestic assault" because the woman is physically attacked by someone she lives with or has lived with at some time. For example, you may have been pushed or shoved, slapped, punched, kicked, choked, or hit with something held in hand, or had something thrown at you by your husband or lover. You may have had your arm twisted and broken or your head banged against a wall. He may have held a knife to you, pointed a gun at you, or actually stabbed or shot you.

There are other kinds of physical abuse you might have experienced that go on in relationships in which a woman is considered to be battered. If he held you, tied you down, or locked you in a room to keep you from leaving; purposely locked you out of the house or left you in a dangerous place; refused to help you when you were sick or injured; drove fast and recklessly when you were in the car with him, actually putting your life in danger in order to frighten you — you have been abused.

Physical abuse can also be sexual in nature. The idea of marital rape is being taken seriously today. Being married to you or living with you does not give a man the right to force sexual relations on you against your wishes. It does not give him the right to insist on sexual practices you find uncomfortable or degrading. A man who hurts you physically during sex; who tries to make you do sexual acts you do not want; who will not stop when you ask; or who threatens to hit you if you do not satisfy his needs, is sexually abusive. *Whenever you have been placed in physical danger or have been controlled by the threat or use of physical force, you have been battered.*

Emotional Abuse

Battered women are also psychologically and emotionally abused. When a man threatens to use physical force against you, whether he actually assaults you or not, he is engaging in psychological battering. A threat in itself is an attack on you. This is especially true if he has hit you before and you are afraid he will do it again. Threats of physical violence take away your sense of safety, security, and well-being. He may also threaten to hurt your children, friends, family, or pets if you do not go along with what he wants. He may actually do them harm, or destroy your property. Threats and actions like these terrorize you and make you feel helpless. You may find yourself forced to go along with what he wants in order to protect yourself or others from his violence.

Physical assault clearly has emotional as well as physical effects. Battered women are often found to have low self-esteem, that is, they don't think very highly of themselves. The pain and fear, the uncertainty, and sense of failure that come from being the victim of repeated physical abuse from someone close to you are emotionally damaging. It's hard to value yourself as a person when someone is using you as a punching bag. Sexually abused women may feel humiliated and ashamed of their bodies. If you are sexually abused, you may become angry and resentful about sex. If you have sexual relations because you are afraid not to or because he keeps at you until you give in, sex becomes an act of power and control over you — not an act of love.

Emotional abuse often takes the form of things said or done apart from physical assault which undermine your self-respect and self-confidence. When your husband or boyfriend curses at you, calls you names and insults you; constantly criticizes you; or embarrasses you in public, he is abusing you emotionally. He may actively belittle you or he may simply ignore your needs and refuse to talk to you or listen to what you have to say. He may be jealous, checking up on everything you do and accusing you of doing things you have not done. If he is trying to control your life, isolating you from other people, telling you you cannot do anything right, and making all your decisions for you, he is being abusive. In battering relationships women take an emotional beating as well as a physical beating.

Consider the cases which are presented in Appendix A. They illustrate the kinds of experiences involving both physical and emotional abuse that battered women face. Your own circumstances may be better or worse, or perhaps better in some ways and worse in others. Every individual situation is different. However, the more you learn about other women's experiences and about battering in general, the better you will understand the underlying similarities. It will still be up to you to decide whether you are in a battering relationship. When you are thinking about your situation, look at your feelings and reactions as well as the specific abusive behaviors that have been directed at you.

Battered women share some common emotional reactions to violence in the home. Do any of the following feelings and thoughts seem familiar? Are you afraid of him? Do you ever think of running away? Do you worry a lot? Do you feel like you cannot relax? Do you always have to be on guard; watching his moods, being careful what you do or say? Do you doubt your judgment and think maybe you are going crazy? Do you think it must be your fault? Do you blame yourself and think that somehow you must deserve to be battered? Have you lost confidence in yourself? Do you feel confused, helpless, or depressed? Do you lack energy or have little interest left for things that used to seem important to you? Have you lost contact with other people; friends, family, co-workers, neighbors? Do you feel like you have no choice but to stay? Do you feel trapped and alone? Any of these feelings are likely reactions to violence in your home.

The Cycle of Violence

Along with growing awareness of the existence of domestic violence as a social problem, there have been efforts to better understand the nature of battering.

In her book, *The Battered Woman*, Lenore Walker talks about the "cycle of violence" as a way of describing what happens in violent relationships between men and women.

Cycle of Violence

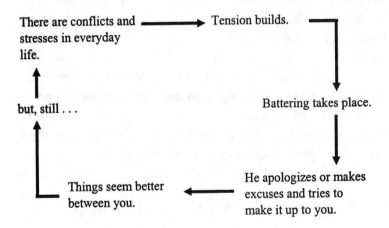

None of us can avoid the conflicts and stresses of everyday life. For the battering man, however, the tensions he experiences as a result of conflict and stress lead to abusive behavior. He explodes in violence that may last just a few minutes or go on for hours, even days. Afterwards he may make excuses or say he is sorry and promise it will not happen again. Maybe he will tell you he loves you and needs you. He may make a special effort to smooth things over by trying to be nice to you. You make up. You forgive and try to forget. You start to minimize the problem. The worst seems over. You think maybe this time it will be different, but you never know for sure. As time goes by conflicts and stresses will come up again. If your partner has not learned new coping behaviors, he will be abusive again.

Shelter workers and family violence researchers see battering as a pattern in a relationship. It is rarely a one-time-only event. Without help, attacks usually increase in number and seriousness. Sometimes it will only take one violent episode, one solid punch or careless shove, to break your jaw; permanently impair your sight or hearing; seriously damage internal organs; give you a concussion; lead to losing the baby if you are pregnant; or hurt someone else in the home. The battering man may or may not intend to do this kind of damage. Later he may say, "I never meant to hurt you so bad." But at the time he is battering, he is not thinking of your safety and you are in danger.

Evaluating Your Relationship

To evaluate the risks in your relationship, you must look carefully at the actual and possible consequences of violent conflicts. How many times have you already been physically abused? How many bruises, cuts, or broken bones did you have as a result? What parts of your body does he most often hurt? Could a much more serious injury have resulted from the same act? For example, if he accidentally hit you a little more to one side, choked you a few seconds longer, or if you fell against a sharp object, would you have survived?

If you have children in the home, how are they doing? There is no doubt that children suffer from battering relationships between adults in the home. Violence creates tension, fear, and uncertainty for all family members who are potential victims. Have your children ever been hurt when they got in the middle of a fight between you and your partner? Has he been abusive to them? Are you worried about their safety and well being? Do you have trouble taking care of the children because of all the conflict at home?

Think, too, about what is happening to your feelings about yourself as a result of the conflict at home. Are you less positive, less confident? Are you unhappy or depressed? How is your general health? Are you experiencing frequent nervous headaches, intestinal or stomach upset, trouble sleeping, or any similar chronic, stress-related health problems? These can be symptoms of an abusive relationship.

If the descriptions you have read here fit your situation, you have been physically, sexually, or emotionally abused — maybe all of these — by the man in your life. Whether you have been tormented emotionally, sexually mistreated, threatened and slapped, or repeatedly assaulted and badly injured, you can answer "yes" to the question raised at the beginning of this chapter. "Yes, I am a battered woman."

Many women resist thinking of themselves as a "battered woman," but if you can see how this term applies to your situation, you will be one step closer to making change possible. You will realize that you are not alone. Many other women have shared your feelings of shock, panic, disgust, anger, sadness, and helplessness when the hand they reach out for is raised in anger against them. They, too, struggle to understand why, and to decide what they should do about being battered. When you look for help from other people you will sometimes be disappointed. However, if you keep trying, you can find the support you need to do what is best for you. In the following chapter we will look at why battering occurs and what alternatives you have.

2
Why Does It Happen?

A woman is raped and people want to know what she was wearing that "turned him on." A woman is beaten by her husband and he tells her that he would not have to do this if she was a good wife. A woman stays with a man who is abusive and others think she must just like being abused. What all these examples have in common is that the woman herself is blamed for what has been done to her. How often have you heard people say, "She asked for it?" Maybe you have thought the same thing. But it is odd, when you think about it, how we blame the victim. Is it really possible to *make* a man rape you? Or beat you? Or insult you? Is it really possible that he has *no choice* but to react this way and *only* this way to the things you say or do? No! A man does make choices in life. He is responsible for his own behavior. No one else *makes* him do what he does. No one forces a man to batter the woman with whom he lives.

You Are Not to Blame

If you are a battered woman, it is very important for you to realize that you do not make it happen. There are conflicts and disagreements in every relationship. When we live with someone else there are always ups and downs. No one is perfect. We have bad moods; we argue; we nag; we make mistakes; we get on each other's nerves and annoy each other. When you do things that annoy the man in your life, he can react in a variety of ways. For example, he can ignore you. He can also leave the house. He can stay and talk to you about what is bothering him. If he hits, that is his choice; his responsibility. You do not "deserve" to be battered; and you are not to blame when he responds to you with violence. Like other battered women, you may still tend to blame yourself because:

- the batterer tells you it is your fault, to justify his behavior;

- others, including friends, relatives, police, judges, social service workers, and counselors, may treat you as though it is your fault; and

- you have probably been raised to believe that women are responsible for making a relationship work; therefore, it is your fault if it goes wrong and it is your job to fix it.

If you think you make the battering happen, then it follows you should also be able to make it stop, by changing your own behavior. What if you try everything you can think of but the abuse still goes on? Consider a battering man who is abusive when dinner is late; the next time he may be abusive because dinner is too early. He yells and curses his wife for going out without telling him; then he insults her for sitting home all day doing nothing. He comes home late and punches her for being asleep; the next time he beats her for waiting up to "spy" on him. If you find yourself in situations like this, as so many battered women do, you have good reason to feel helpless and confused. If nothing you do seems to work it is because what you do is not what makes him abusive in the first place. *You cannot prevent the abuse because you do not actually cause it!*

When you think about your own relationship, ask yourself the following questions: Does his anger seem way out of proportion to what you have actually said or done? When other things are getting to him, are you the one he takes it out on? Did you ever feel that he was just looking for an excuse to start a fight? Do the reasons he gives for acting this way seem unfair or not make sense to you? Is he abusive no matter what you do to please him? Do you feel that he will never be satisfied, no matter what you do? To live up to his demands, would you have to be someone very different than the person you really are? If so, you can see that his behavior is not something you make happen. Battered women are sometimes harder on themselves than anyone. Maybe you think you are a difficult person to live with. Perhaps you are! However, this does not give him the right to batter you.

One of the problems you will face is that many people still accept the idea that battered women "bring it on themselves." A great deal of harm is done by this attitude. If you blame yourself for the bad things that are happening to you, your feelings of self-worth are lowered even more. Also, when the victim is blamed in cases of woman battering, the man is allowed to avoid taking responsibility for his behavior. When your abusive partner blames you and other people seem to agree, he has an excuse for not changing. Instead, you are expected to stop the abuse somehow. Taking the responsibility and blaming yourself for something you cannot change will add to your sense of confusion, frustration, and failure. Accepting a false belief about what causes battering lessens your ability to understand what is actually happening and may lead you to spend a lot of time and effort on ineffective solutions.

Of course you play a part in the battering relationship, but you do not make him hit and you alone cannot make him stop. That is something he must do for himself. When you can be clear about this in your own mind, you will be better able to make decisions for yourself and be better prepared to stand your ground when the batterer or people outside the relationship try to blame you.

The Battering Society

Abusive, battering men come from every kind of social background. Family violence is not limited by race, religion, or ethnic origin. The man who batters may have dropped out of high school or he may have completed an advanced college degree. He might be unemployed or working full-time. Even highly respected professionals — doctors, lawyers, business executives, professors, ministers — are known to assault their wives. The battering of women is too common to be considered just the personal problem of a few "sick" men. It is a much larger social problem.

Violence is sometimes passed on from one generation to the next in homes where battering takes place. Children first learn about the adult world in their families. If children grow up in a home with woman battering or child abuse they may learn that:

- violence in the home is a useful way to deal with conflict;
- being a man means you can use physical force against a woman;
- being a woman means being a victim; and
- discipline rightly includes physically or verbally attacking another member of the family.

Children do not necessarily get the message that this is the way family life should be, but they may come away with the idea that this is how it is. In later life, many men from violent or abusive homes repeat in their own behavior, sometimes consciously and sometimes without meaning to, the patterns they observed in childhood.

Violence runs throughout our society, and women are often the target. In part, this results from the way men and women are raised. Men are encouraged to be strong, independent, aggressive, and competitive. Men are expected to take charge and to be in control, of the situation and of themselves. They are taught that they should provide for a woman economically, and learn to expect sex and deference from her in return. Traditionally, the man is boss. Women are taught to be more passive, cooperative, dependent, and nurturing. Women are expected to be more emotional, less rational. They are regarded as "the weaker sex." In return for his protection, a woman is expected to "stand by her man" and make him feel as if he is the "king of his castle," their home.

Who then protects the woman when her protector turns against her in acts of violence? Our society has been slow to recognize the problem of wife beating. In the past, laws and common practice encouraged husbands to discipline their wives, by force, if they saw fit. Even today, the courts and the community often hesitate to get involved in what is seen as a private matter between husbands and wives. Society has failed to protect the battered woman from her abusive partner and has made it difficult for her to leave him. Attitudes that favor keeping the family together at all costs work against battered women. Continuing inequalities in work and educational opportunities make it difficult for women to be economically independent, especially when they have children.

Despite recent changes brought about as a result of the Women's Movement, in many ways it is still "a man's world." Overall, men dominate our society. They hold more positions of power outside the home and often have an attitude of superiority. This attitude leads to putting women down, taking their ideas less seriously, and not respecting their abilities. Sometimes the effect is that women feel bad about themselves without really knowing why. There is no one offending person or situation you can single out; somehow "it's just the way things are."

But attitudes are changing. Research on family violence has made clear that the problem of battered women in our society is too widespread to ignore or to successfully explain away by blaming the victim. Since the 1970s there has been increased awareness of domestic assault. As a result many new resources are available. Shelters are being established to provide safety from immediate physical harm for battered women and their children. Other services include continuing efforts to educate the public on the problem of domestic violence. If you are a battered woman, you are no longer alone. Today, more than ever, help is available.

Percentage of Persons Physically Assaulted by an Intimate Partner in Lifetime by Type of Assault and Sex of Victim[a]

Type of Assault	Women (n=8,000)	Men (n=8,000)
Total physical assault by intimate partner[b]	**22.1**	**7.4**
Threw something[b]	8.1	4.4
Pushed, grabbed, shoved[b]	18.1	5.4
Pulled hair[b]	9.1	2.3
Slapped, hit[b]	16.0	5.5
Kicked, bit[b]	5.5	2.6
Choked, tried to drown[b]	6.1	0.5
Hit with object[b]	5.0	3.2
Beat up[b]	8.5	0.6
Threatened with gun[b]	3.5	0.4
Threatened with knife[b]	2.8	1.6
Used gun[b]	0.7	0.1
Used knife	0.9	0.8

[a]Intimate partner includes current or former spouses, opposite-sex cohabiting partners, same-sex cohabiting partners, dates, and boyfriends/girlfriends.
[b]Differences between women and men are statistically significant: p-value < .001.

Source: *Research in Brief.* National Institute of Justice, U.S. Department of Justice, November 1998.

3
The Battering Man

A battered woman will often continue to feel a sense of attachment and obligation to her partner. She remains concerned about his welfare. She tries to understand the battering man. She may stay with him in the hope that he will change. What about the batterer? Why does he do it? Will he change? People who have worked with and studied men who batter have made several observations which are especially important for you to consider.

What Do Battering Men Have in Common?

Although each case is unique, the following characteristics appear to be common among men who batter:

Low self-esteem. Though he may present a different picture to outsiders, within himself a battering man is likely to feel insecure and unsure of himself. If you live with a battering man, you may have noticed how much he talks himself up. If he really feels so good about himself, why is he working so hard to try to convince everyone else? Because you live together you may see him at some of his weakest moments and he may be afraid you will use this against him. If he feels bad about himself, getting close to you — which means letting you see his faults — is threatening. He may get angry at you because he feels afraid.

Traditional sex-role expectations. Many men and women still believe that a man should be the head of the household and have the final say in family decisions. What sets the battering man apart, however, is that his expecta-tions are very demanding, rigid, and unbending. He will be angry if you cannot live up to his idea of what a wife or girlfriend should be — a task which may be impossible for anyone to do. He may also feel like a failure, and take his anger out on you, if he cannot be the kind of man he thinks he should be.

No matter how much you try to live up to his expecta-tions, it will not be good enough. No matter how hard you try to reassure him, he will still be unsure of himself. You may think that all he needs is the love of a good woman to change him. Unfortunately, this is not true for the battering man. It is important for you to understand that his problems reflect long-time feelings the batterer has about himself, feelings with which he must come to terms. You cannot fix them!

Jealous and controlling. Jealousy at first may seem flattering. You may think that he wouldn't be jealous if he did not care. However, the batterer's jealousy is extreme. It reflects not so much his caring but rather his insecurity. What kind of caring is it when he checks up on you con-stantly? What kind of caring is it when he wants to decide where you go, when you go, who you see? In the batterer, jealousy and the desire to be in control are especially dan-gerous because he feels he has a right to control you with physical force. He justifies his action to himself on the basis of things he thinks you have done "wrong" to make him jealous or to defy him. "Defying" him might mean anything you do to be independent or to think for yourself — anything that is not what he wants. How can you do only what he wants and still be your own person? If you are passive and cooperative to please him, you may begin to lose your sense of yourself as a separate individual in your own right. You may get out of practice making decisions for yourself. But if you try to assert yourself, the battering man often feels threatened and becomes abusive.

Abusive family backgrounds. Though not all men who were raised in abusive homes become batterers, many battering men grew up in violent homes. They either observed their fathers abuse their mothers or were themselves victims of child abuse. These kinds of early experiences affect a child's emotional development and adult personality; they can undermine basic feelings of security, safety, trust, love, and belonging. A violent family background also teaches violent behavior as a response to stress and fails to provide a model of more constructive ways to deal with conflict in a relationship. Typically, the battering man has not developed positive ways to communicate his feelings and needs or the ability to make necessary compromises. His unmet needs and negative feelings from childhood are sometimes overpowering and, basically, he regards his violence as an acceptable way to express himself because he sees no effective alternatives.

While knowing he has this kind of background may help you understand why he does what he does, *it does not excuse him.* If you care about him, you probably feel sorry for him. You want to be understanding. You may come to see him as a victim too. Still, this does not give him the

right to batter you. Being sympathetic and understanding of
him as a person does not mean you must accept his abusive
behavior.

Blames others. Battering men will typically blame everyone and everything but themselves for their actions. As
discussed earlier, the battering man will often blame you.
While you may want to try to convince him that you are not
at fault, your arguments will probably not do much good.
What you can do is to be sure that *you* know that you are
not the cause of the problem. Whenever you start to doubt
yourself, re-read the section in Chapter 2 about blaming the
victim. Remember, *you* are responsible for your own actions; *you* are not responsible for his abusive behavior.

A battering man will blame other people too — his
boss, his customers or co-workers who irritate him; friends
who don't come through for him; family members who
make demands on him; and outsiders who try to tell him
what to do. An abusive man has a lot of trouble dealing
with everyday stresses. When things go wrong, his already-
low sense of self-worth is threatened, and his need to feel in
control is increased. He may also believe that because you
are his wife or girlfriend you are supposed to make him feel
better. When you cannot, he strikes out at you. The "reasons" he gives may be all of the things that have happened
to him that "make" him explode this way. But the real reason is within himself. Violence is the way he has learned to
react to stress. Violence is the way he has learned to regain
a sense of control.

Uses Alcohol and Other Drugs as an Excuse. In some
abusive relationships the battering man also has problems
with alcohol or other drugs. If so, both he and the woman
he batters are likely to mistakenly blame his abusive behav-

ior on his drinking or other drug use. For example, he may say: "I wouldn't have hit you if I wasn't high; I didn't know what I was doing." She may think, "He still loves me; he only gets like that when he's had too much to drink." What's wrong with these kinds of explanations? They are an attempt to explain violence away as if the man is not responsible for what he does. When you focus on the alcohol or other drugs you fail to deal directly with the problem of battering itself.

Denial. Have you ever wondered how your partner can do the kinds of things that he does to you and still expect you to go on as if nothing happened? Does he seem to forget the many times when he has been physically violent or verbally abusive? When you or others bring up these times, does he ever make light of them? He may say: "I didn't do that;" "It wasn't that bad;" "Anyone can have a bad day;" "You are just as bad;" "Why are you making such a fuss?;" "I only hit you three times;" or "So and so gets much worse." Another form of denial is when a man talks a lot about his past violence and about what he will do to you the next time, almost as if he is bragging about his violence. In this case, too, he is failing to understand how serious and inappropriate the use of violence is in a personal relationship.

Denial is very common among battering men. They do not want to face the seriousness of their behavior and its consequences. Sometimes they will lie about things they remember but do not want to admit, especially to outsiders. Denial often goes deeper. Battering men also lie to *themselves* to avoid feeling their victim's pain, terror, or injury. They may be quick to apologize and want to make up with the women they are hurting. However, they are just as quick to forget what they have done and will get angry if they are reminded. They expect their victims to understand and forgive their abusive behavior. At the same time they will be unable or unwilling to see how much their violence physically and emotionally hurts their victims.

Fails to Accept the Need for Change. Because the battering man blames others for his own actions and denies the seriousness of what he has done, and because men in our society often feel they have a right to do whatever they want in their own home, the battering man typically *does not believe his abusive behavior should have negative consequences.* He is going to put a lot of pressure on you — direct and roundabout — to convince you of this. He will try to charm you, manipulate you, and threaten you. If you take any action against him because of his abusiveness, he may act surprised and even hurt. "Why are you doing this to me?" he may say. It's a very difficult position for you to be in. Your man may be one of the most important people in your life and have a strong influence on the way you see yourself and your relationship. Keep in mind, though, that he is looking to protect himself. What you are going through is not just happening to you. Every battering man whose partner has decided to say "no" to an abusive relationship has probably tried to convince her — using much the same line — that there is nothing wrong, at least nothing that can't be worked out between the two of them.

Will He Ever Change?

The philosophy of most counseling programs for battering men is that violence is a learned reaction, and that alternatives — other, more constructive ways to deal with conflict and stress — can be learned. Counselors believe abusive men are responsible for taking the steps necessary to change their behavior. Battering men need to learn to talk more openly about themselves, their feelings, and their home situations. They need to overcome denial and ask for help. They need to learn that even when they are angry they do not have to hit. They need to actively try other ways of dealing with conflict and stress to find those that work best for them. Above all, they need to realize that their battering behavior is unacceptable and they must be willing to change.

If you have lived with a battering man you probably have some idea how hard taking such steps would be for him. Based on what you have read here about what battering men have in common and what you know from past experience with your own partner, how likely do you think it is that he will change?

Some men do change. Most do not. Current estimates are that nine out of 10 batterers do not believe they need to end their abusive behavior. Relatively few abusive men take part in counseling programs. Some join "voluntarily" when their wives or girlfriends have left them or are preparing to leave; some join only when forced to by the courts after arrest and conviction for domestic assault. Of those men who do go for counseling, many drop out. Others stay in a counseling program but refuse to change. Change is never easy for these men. Outside pressure is necessary, but not enough. The longer the battering has gone on and the more the man has been abusive in other relationships with women, the less likely it is that he will change.

A Word of Caution

If you are looking for something to hold on to, you are probably hoping that the man who batters you will change. Counseling for the man who is abusive, if he will go, may seem like the answer. Be careful how much trust you put in this. Often a man goes for counseling, without any real commitment to change, simply to get his wife or girlfriend to stay with him or to come back to him. Now he can say, "Give me another chance. Look, I am really trying. You can't walk out on me now." Try to be as realistic and objective as you can. He has probably made promises before that he didn't keep. Try not to believe only what you want to believe.

It is very important for you to realize that his going to counseling, in itself, does *not* guarantee your safety. Judge your own situation by what actually goes on when you are together. Judge his actions as well as this words. Is he telling you he has changed but still acting as he did before? Is the abuse just taking a different form now? What, specifically, is different now? You may find it helpful to make a list of what he used to say or do that he doesn't say or do anymore, and another list of what he is saying or doing now that he didn't say or do before. List both good and bad behaviors. Do you really feel safe with him? No matter how sincere he may seem to be in wanting to change, the only safe way for you to judge your situation is by whether or not the battering actually stops.

4
What Can I Do?

Battering has serious consequences for everyone involved: for the man who does not get help, the woman he hurts, and the children who live in the shadow of a violent home. The futures of children depend for the most part upon decisions made by the adults in their lives. If battering men do not see themselves as having a problem, they will not change; so, what can a battered woman do?

You Have Options and Opportunities

While you cannot control the batterer, you can decide how to respond to his abusive behavior. That much is within your power. You have various options. For example, you can stay in the abusive relationship and continue doing what you have been doing. You can stay in the relationship and try something different to make it better, with or without outside help. You can leave temporarily or seek permanent separation. Every woman who finds herself in an abusive relationship must decide what she will do about her own unique situation. If you have been emotionally beaten down by repeated abuse you may come to believe that there is nothing you can do. When you have hoped that things would change but have been disappointed so many times before, it is hard to believe that things will ever be different. Battered women often feel a sense of hopelessness and despair which leads them to resign themselves to their "fate." If this has happened to you, you may be overlooking options and opportunities to make your life better, with your partner or without him.

Become More Self-aware

First, it will help if you can recognize that no matter how helpless you may feel, you are already making choices for yourself. Look at how you have been dealing with your situation up to now. How do you react to your partner's abusive behavior? What do you do? What do you *not* do? Were there ever times that you thought of a number of different things you might say or do and then picked one over the others? Have you ever thought of doing something but then decided not to do it because it would be too much trouble, too embarrassing, too risky, or wouldn't work? Every day you make decisions and choices you may not be aware of, or that seem so small and unimportant that you don't count them. Give yourself credit, count them! The battering man may limit the control you have over your life, but you are not helpless. *You can and do act on your own.*

Now, consider the choices you have made so far in your life. Ask yourself how satisfied you are with the results and whether or not you might want to do things differently. What are the advantages and drawbacks of the decisions you've made so far? How much longer are you willing to live with the situation as it is now? What risks are you taking if you stay? If you leave? It is important to see yourself as more than a victim. While the batterer is responsible for his abusive behavior, you are responsible for the choices you make. You do have the power to make certain decisions about your life. You can make positive changes. Still, change is not easy! You may have to ask for help. The title of this book, *You Are Not Alone*, is meant to let you know that you can find help, if you look for it.

Take Care of Yourself

While you are deciding what kind of help to seek, there is much you can do to take care of yourself and gain greater control over your life.

Plan what to do in an emergency. Think ahead about what you can do if your husband or boyfriend is violent in the future. For example, memorize the local emergency numbers which you might need. Put a little money aside for food, telephone calls, and transportation in case you have to leave home for a day or two. Figure out where you can go to stay and how you will get there. Have an overnight bag already packed for you and your children; leave it with someone else if that would be safer for you. If possible, keep small valuables and important papers — birth certificates, drivers license, social security cards, medical records, bank books and so on — all together some place where you can easily get to them if you have to leave the house in a hurry. Keep a spare set of house keys and car keys handy. Think ahead about different ways you might be able to get yourself and your children out of the house. The more you plan and practice what to do ahead of time, the easier it will be for you to react in an emergency.

Keep records. Get a notebook, diary or calendar and start keeping a record of times you have been battered. As soon after an abusive incident as possible, *write down* what happened, where and when, and how you felt. Keep a record of all injuries to yourself or the children. Note whether you went to the doctor or hospital for treatment, and whether there were any other witnesses. This may seem like a bother, but it will help prove how much battering there is in your relationship — to yourself, if you are minimizing the abuse, and to the courts, if you seek divorce or have the batterer arrested.

Consider your long-term prospects. Start thinking about what kinds of skills you would need to be more independent. If you need additional education or job training, try to get started now with at least a part-time job or a few high school or college credits. If you can find a time in the cycle of violence when your partner is most willing to go along with what you want, take advantage of that time to start new activities. Even if he resists at first, after a while your partner may adjust to whatever you are doing. If he is going to batter you anyway, no matter what you do, you may as well keep at it so you will be better prepared to leave. However, if you see that he is becoming more abusive and you do not want to risk getting hurt, don't feel guilty about "quitting." Do what you think is best and safest for you now, but keep making plans for the future.

Imagine life without him. Begin to picture what you would do if something happened to him and he was not around for you anymore. Think about what steps you would go through, day by day, to cope with life on your own. As you do this you will probably picture some very serious difficulties that you don't know how to handle. Think about them one by one as if you were going through an obstacle course. To get to the finish line you have to figure out some ways to get under, over, or around each obstacle. Talk to other people and find out how they have handled similar situations. Slowly, you will be better able to imagine yourself getting through all kinds of difficulties and surviving. This exercise will help you come up with new ideas and will increase your self-confidence.

Talk to other people. Don't let yourself be isolated. Make an effort to keep in touch with family members, friends, neighbors. Spend time with other people so that you do not have to depend completely on the battering man for emotional support. Look for people whose company you enjoy, and who encourage you to feel better about yourself. It might be someone you can talk to about the battering; it might be someone with whom you can share other things. The more you are involved in activities and relationships outside of home, the more opportunities you will have to feel like an individual in your own right, with good qualities and something to offer others.

Be careful who you tell. If you are *sure* your husband or boyfriend would be more cooperative and less abusive if he knew of your plans to be more independent and to get outside support, you may want to tell him. Keep in mind that battering men typically feel insecure about themselves and in his own way your batterer is dependent on you. He is likely to feel very anxious and threatened by the idea that you are planning to spend more time away from him, no matter how abusive he has been. The more he knows about your plans, the easier it may be for him to stop you from doing what you need to do for yourself.

Seek Help Early

Be open to admitting to yourself that you are in a battering relationship. Do not expect the problem to go away or solve itself. Suppose you have one argument in which your husband or boyfriend strikes you in anger or to "teach you a lesson." If this is the first time it is very likely that you do not know quite what to make of it. Maybe it will never happen again, and maybe everyone deserves a second chance. If it does happen again, even after some time has gone by, do not let yourself overlook the pattern which is emerging. Discuss the situation with your partner. See if you can get him to understand that even if you make mistakes and he gets angry he cannot keep hitting you. You can make some compromises and changes too, but he must work on other ways to handle conflicts to your relationship. If he is not able or willing to see this, take it as another warning sign of trouble ahead.

Start talking to other people when the first abusive incidents occur. If you think it might help, have neighbors, friends, or relatives talk to your partner and encourage him to get help before a long-term pattern of serious battering is established. Your partner might be more willing to own up to his actions if he has not yet gone too far. For many kinds of family problems — like incest, alcoholism, or battering — the culturally reinforced tendency toward secrecy and denial makes things much worse in the long run. It is tragic that so many women suffer years of abuse and terror before breaking through the wall of silence that separates them from outside help. The reactions battered women get from outsiders are not always positive and constructive. However, if you can anticipate some of the problems you may encounter, it will be easier to overcome them.

5
Neighbors, Family, and Friends

Neighbors, family, and friends can be important resources for you if you are a battered woman. They cannot do everything and may not always be there for you when you need them, but sometimes they can be very helpful. The better you understand what your needs are, the easier it will be for you to determine how neighbors, family, and friends might be able to help you.

Identifying Your Needs

Try making a list of your needs. A very general list might include: safety, shelter, emotional support, advice, referral, and financial assistance. More specific needs under each category could be listed too. For example, under the heading of safety, you might need a way to get out of the house quickly when a physical assault begins or a ride to the hospital if you are injured. For shelter, you might need a place to stay for a few days while you think about what to do next. For emotional support, you might need someone to simply listen or someone who will actively encourage you to have more confidence in yourself and explore different ways of responding to the abuse you have experienced. And so on. The more specific you can be, the better you will know what kinds of assistance to look for from others.

If you have trouble making a list like this you may need to start by getting help in identifying your needs. You may have spent so much time thinking about and trying to meet other people's needs that it is hard to recognize your own. Take some time out to focus on yourself. You deserve this attention. It is not a weakness to admit that you need help. Rather, it is an important step in taking care of yourself. Once you have identified your needs, you are ready to think about the resources available to help you meet these needs.

Neighbors

If you are a battered woman you have probably tried to keep the abuse a secret and have not admitted what is going on to neighbors. You may not want them to know for fear of what they will think, say, or do. You may be trying to protect your family's reputation and respectability. It is not unusual for battered women to be inhibited by feelings of guilt, shame, embarrassment, failure, and self-blame. The battering man certainly will not encourage you to make any kind of public disclosure. You may also believe that domestic quarrels are a private family matter in which outsiders should not interfere.

Because neighbors are physically close, they are likely to see or hear some evidence of battering. Even when they know about the battering they may not volunteer to help you. Neighbors may be embarrassed or worried about their safety. They may feel that they already have enough problems of their own and do not have time to get involved. Even if they are willing to do something, they may not know exactly what to do and they may not be sure you want them to help.

If you are willing to ask, there are certain kinds of help neighbors can provide that require only limited involvement on their part. For example, a neighbor could:

- keep a spare set of keys for you;

- babysit for an hour or two;

- take you to the hospital or to a doctor in an emergency;

- call the police.

Neighbors can sometimes help without needing to know the exact reasons behind your request. Other times you will have to tell more about your situation. For example, suppose you want your neighbors to call the police the next time you are being battered. Without going into all the details of your family problems you can let them know what kind of help you need by saying something like, "Maybe you have heard some of the arguments that go on at our place. Mostly I would rather not get outsiders involved, but if this (explain what you have in mind) ever happens, please go ahead and call the police." If neighbors say they are not interested, you will know in advance that you need to turn to someone else.

Family

A place to stay, away from the battering man, is one of the critical needs battered women have in common. Parents are the people to whom battered women most often turn for shelter. The poet Robert Frost wrote that "home is the place that when you have to go there, they have to take you in." Parents are often willing to take a daughter in, at least for a short period of time. If your parents refuse, it may be because of unsympathetic attitudes or because of practical limitations of inadequate space and strained finances. The expense and inconvenience of traveling may also be a problem if your parents do not live close by. Nevertheless, keep parents and other relatives in mind when you need shelter.

Relatives can be helpful too when you need someone to talk to about your home situation. Parents are usually the first persons a battered woman will tell about the abuse at home. Relatives are people you can tell and still "keep it in the family." Parents, especially, are socially defined as people who will give aid and comfort when their children, even as adults, are in trouble.

Still, it is not always easy to go to parents. It can be embarrassing to tell them that the man you chose to live with is abusive. Especially if you are blaming yourself, it seems like you, not the batterer, are admitting failure. Because marriage implies a shift in loyalty from your original family to your new partner by marriage, you may feel you are being disloyal or childish to turn back to your parents. Also, parents may encourage emotional dependence on them at a time when it is important for you to learn to be more independent. Another kind of problem occurs when parents put conditions on their help that you are not willing to accept (e.g., "Divorce him or quit complaining to us," or, "We will give you a loan for school but only if you go back to him and try again."). You will have to try to convince them that you need their help but also need room to make your own decisions.

Sometimes your parents will have attitudes that are not supportive. For instance, they may not believe that things at home are as bad as you say, or they may think that what is happening is your fault. They may believe in keeping a marriage together no matter what; "After all, he is still a good provider, doesn't hit the kids," and so on. Because of their own upbringing they may not be willing to discuss sexual aspects of abuse with you. Finally, parents may be genuinely concerned about you but, like neighbors, uncertain or confused about exactly what they should do to help you. Unlike neighbors, parents are apt to react more strongly, for better or worse, because they are more emotionally involved in what happens to you.

In spite of possible complications, parents and other family members are an important resource. Do not let your own embarrassment keep you from going to them if you really want or need their help. Tell them a little at a time about what has been going on if you have been keeping it a secret up to now. Be sure to give them time to get over their initial shock and disbelief. Remember how difficult it has been for *you* to accept the reality of the battering relationship even though you experienced it firsthand. Give them something to read about woman battering. This book or one of the other suggested titles would help them understand the larger problem of domestic assault and could make talking to them about your own situation easier.

Family members may still have some attitudes that are not supportive. If most of your life they always managed to say the "wrong" thing when you went to them for help, this time probably will not be different. When going to relatives consider what kind of support they are best able to offer. If you have some idea what your needs are, let them know what kind of assistance you want. For example, "I need a place to stay for a short time, please no questions now," or, "You don't have to do anything, I just need to talk to someone who will listen, and not think I am crazy." Different family members may be able to provide assistance in different ways. One may be uncomfortable talking about the battering but willing to help you out financially. Another, who is not able to take you in, may still be able to take time out to listen and provide emotional support.

Friends

The more you are cut off from outside support, the more vulnerable you are to emotional manipulation by the batterer. Having friends you can trust to talk to about your home situation — friends who will believe you and will not blame you or reject you — is an important counterforce when you are in an abusive relationship. The saying, "A friend is someone who knows all about you and likes you anyway," captures the kind of openness and acceptance a good friend can provide. Just being able to talk to a sympathetic listener can help to clarify in your own mind what is happening at home.

Friends may have a variety of reactions, depending on their own attitudes and biases. They are likely to have their own points of view about what you "should" or "should not" do. The feedback they give you, whether you agree with what they say or not, can provide new ideas. Listen to their suggestions, but recognize that you do not have to accept them as right for you. Try to explore with your friends as many possible ways of looking at and dealing with the abusive relationship as you can think of together.

It may be difficult telling a friend for the first time about an abusive relationship because you never know for sure how he or she will react. Sometimes friends will have already guessed and will be relieved that by bringing the subject up you have given them permission to talk about it. Some friends, for reasons of their own, will be very uncomfortable with the whole idea and will not want to get into it with you. If this is because they are nervous and uncertain about how they should react, it will smooth the way if you can give them some idea of what kind of help you would like from them. For example, friends can help you escape to a shelter, give you a small loan, go with you to see a lawyer, or just spend time with you when you need company. If you talk to friends about the battering, give them some time, too, to think about what you have told them. You may not get the reaction you want at first, but they may come around later when they understand the situation better. Otherwise you should just accept the fact that some friends will not be able to give you the kind of help you need. Keep in mind that this is their limitation and not your fault.

Acquaintances

Do not let yourself give up on finding someone to talk to about the battering — whether it is a sympathetic neighbor, relative, or friend. Also, do not overlook acquaintances as resource persons. An acquaintance might be someone you see once a week in an exercise class, a co-worker, the mother of one of your children's playmates, a teacher of yours, or a member of your church. Acquaintances may not know you as well as family, friends, or neighbors but they may be more knowledgeable or understanding about the subject of battering. To find out, try bringing up the subject of battering in a very general way — for example, by mentioning a book or newspaper article you read, a show you saw on television, or a conversation you had with someone else on battering — and ask the person you are talking to now what he or she thinks. Acquaintances may be able to provide you with general information, new ideas that will apply to your own situation and how to handle it, and some emotional support, whether you ever tell them about your own situation or not.

It is wise to be realistic in your expectations when you approach neighbors, family, friends, or acquaintances for help. Some will be indifferent; some will even be hostile. Such reactions are sometimes very painful and always disappointing. It helps to see this as a reflection of their own limitations and not as a personal failing on your part. Sometimes people will say the wrong things and let you down because they really do not understand about battering. However, sometimes you will get help and support from unexpected sources, if you let people know you need their help and support. You cannot be sure, until you take the chance of asking, just how willing and able others are to provide temporary shelter, emotional support, financial assistance, general information, or whatever else you may need.

Combining Informal Resources

Because you are likely to have a variety of different needs, you should consider all of the resources available to you. Combining different resources to help meet your needs makes it less likely you will hesitate to ask for fear of "imposing" too much on any one person. Of course, it means taking more risks initially, but the more people you can turn to when you are in trouble, the more likely it is that someone will come through for you.

The Battering Man's Reaction

An abusive partner is not likely to be pleased when you develop outside interests and relationships. We have already noted in Chapter 3 that battering men have in common a tendency to be jealous and controlling. If your partner expects you to be always available to meet his needs, he may see neighbors, family, and friends, or even acquaintances, as causing you to neglect him. A battering man is apt to be suspicious and resentful of other persons with whom you share your time and feelings. Partly, this reflects the kinds of personal insecurities he feels. Partly, it reflects the strong motivation he has to conceal his behavior from others.

A battering man may be openly hostile to your neighbors, family, or friends to try to drive them away. Or, he may be very charming and manipulative to convince others that nothing is wrong, so if you talk to them they will think you must be lying or exaggerating the problem. He will almost certainly find ways to make it difficult for you to maintain outside relationships; for example, by complaining, sulking, finding fault with the other people you know, threatening you, or physically restraining you. You may find yourself drifting away from contact with other people because it does not seem worth the struggle you have to go through to maintain these relationships in the face of your partner's resistance.

You are also fighting against a cultural expectation that a couple, especially a married couple, should turn inward and rely only on one another to meet all their needs. It may help if you recognize that not only for you but for most of us this is a completely unrealistic expectation. For the battered woman, especially, it adds unfairly to the burden of guilt that keeps her from seeking help. An abusive relationship by its very nature cannot possibly be meeting all your needs and you have a right to seek outside support. Do not assume that the best or only way to deal with your problems is all by yourself. Contacts with neighbors, family, friends, and acquaintances are worth the effort. Making and keeping up such contacts are part of what you can do for yourself if you are a battered woman.

It is important to remember, however, that neighbors, family, friends, and acquaintances cannot stop the battering. Only the batterer can do that. When outsiders get involved in trying to help you they will rarely try to change your abusive partner's behavior themselves. More likely, they will try to help you find a way to cope with or free yourself from his violence. The problem, in other words, will be treated as your problem, not his. The batterer will usually be avoided.

Outsiders worry about becoming targets of violence themselves if they confront the battering man directly. Instead they leave you and your children to face him. Outsiders know that they cannot be there all the time to stop him from abusing you and they worry about making the situation worse for you if they say the wrong thing to him.

They may share the belief that it is not really "proper" to meddle in other people's family matters.

The batterer will be quick to remind your neighbors, family, and friends that what goes on in his own home is nobody else's business. If they do try to talk to the abusive man about his behavior they may be frustrated or turned away by his denials and unlikely excuses, even in the face of obvious evidence of battering. Or they may be taken in, either by his denials or by his promises to change. You can help prepare neighbors, family, or friends who are willing to confront the batterer by telling them how you think he might react. They cannot make him stop battering, but they can at least let the batterer know that his behavior is not "right."

As a society, we have only recently come to understand and deal with the problem of spouse abuse. This has happened largely through efforts to develop shelters and programs for battered women. The problem of woman battering remains your problem, not because you create it, but because we as a society still do not deal effectively with the man who is battering you. Realistically, then, if you are a battered woman it will be up to you to seek help. Shelters and programs for battered women are available today as a resource to help you find a way to deal with being in a relationship with a man who batters.

6
Why Contact a Shelter?

Shelters for battered women are probably the single most valuable resource you have outside of family and friends. Shelters for battered women offer many services that will be of use to you.

- Someplace safe to go to get away from physical assault at home.
- People who will listen and understand what you are going through.
- Counseling to help you sort out your feelings and decide what to do about the battering.
- Crisis lines you can call for help.
- Support groups in which you can talk to other battered women.
- Programs to help your children deal better with the battering.
- Educational workshops on a variety of topics of interest.

- Written materials that will help you understand why battering happens and what you can do about it.

- Advocacy — people who will stand up for you.

- Information about other kinds of help you can get in your community — medical, legal, and social services.

Contacting a shelter is part of what you can do for yourself if you are a battered woman. Consider the needs you have. How might a shelter or program for battered women be able to help you?

Refuge

Shelters provide a safe place to go in an emergency situation. Most shelters offer transportation so that you and your children can escape from immediate physical danger. Shelters keep a supply of food and clothing on hand so that if you have to leave home in a hurry you will still have food to eat and clothes to wear. While you are at the shelter you will be protected from abuse. You will have a place to stay, away from the pressures of home, where you can think over what to do next. Even if you never actually use the shelter in your area as a place to stay, it helps to know it is there. It is an option that is available to you. You do not have to take a beating at home just because there is no place to go.

Understanding

Shelter workers know that battering does happen. They will believe you. They will listen; they will not judge you or blame you. Many battered women who go to a shelter are surprised to find that shelter workers can sometimes describe what is going on in the battering relationship even before hearing all the specific details of a particular case. Staff at shelters for battered women have had enough contact with women in abusive relationships to be aware of their common experiences. They know the right questions to ask. This means that when you contact a shelter for battered women you will have someone to confide in who is already sensitive to the dynamics of battering, including the behavior of the batterer, the effects of battering on female victims, and the typical reactions of outsiders. Counselors at a shelter are familiar with battered women's worries, conflicts, and confusions. They will understand your experiences and needs.

Counseling

Counseling is also provided at shelters. Trained counselors will help you explore your feelings about your home situation and the effects that battering has had on you.

What you tell counselors at a shelter is private and confidential. Shelter workers will not tell the batterer or anyone else that you called if you do not want anyone else to know. They are trained to be able to help you sort out your feelings and decide for yourself what you want to do; not to take over and tell you how to run your life or talk you into doing things that you do not want to do.

Counselors will help you identify your own personal strengths and encourage your sense of self-worth and self-respect. They will help you find a solution that is right for you and give you support in following through on whatever actions you decide to take. They can help you coordinate

your use of other resources and advise you step-by-step as
you work things out. With their support you do not have to
go through it all alone.

Crisis Lines

Perhaps the most widely used service that shelters for
battered women offer is the 24-hour crisis line. With a 24-
hour crisis line, trained volunteers are available to answer
telephone calls any time of the day or night. You do not
have to go to the shelter, now or in the future, to make use
of the crisis line. You can call as often as you want. If you
sense growing tension at home and see signs that your partner is beginning to lose control or if you feel panicky and
are not sure what to do — call the crisis line.

If you want to get away to a safe place to avoid an assault, or if you have been injured and need help — call the
crisis line. If your partner has been arrested and you do not
know what you should do next — call the crisis line. If you
have the impulse to call and, for the first time, tell someone
that you are a battered woman — call the crisis line. Even if
you simply want general information about battering or
services available to battered women, you can call. Friends
or relatives who want to talk about what is happening to a
battered woman they know, without revealing her identity,
can call for advice. If you have already turned to other people for help and are getting mixed messages — something
about their reaction makes you uncomfortable but you are
not quite sure what it is — call and discuss it. If you are
feeling upset or depressed, call. Do not hesitate to call even
if there is no immediate danger of a physical assault. A
"crisis" can be any turning point in your life when you

want to reach out to others for help. Hearing someone's voice at the other end provides some reassurance that you do not have to face the problem of battering all alone.

Opportunity to Talk to Other Battered Women

Another important benefit of contacting a shelter is the opportunity to meet other women who have been battered and to learn about their experiences. Some women have been in relationships where the battering will sound worse than anything you have experienced so far. You are likely to find, though, that all the women you talk to share some common concerns. At times they all felt hopeless, but they kept trying. They found some of the support and encouragement they needed at the shelter.

Shelters encourage women to form "support groups." In support groups, women who have stayed at the shelter and other women from the community who have been battered can get together on a regular basis and talk about how they have tried to deal with their home situation. They can discuss what has been helpful to them and what has not. Women who have left their partners and women who are staying with their partners can compare experiences. Newcomers in the group are able to talk with other battered women who have already come a long way in coping with the effects of an abusive relationship. Women who have been in the group longer come to recognize how much progress they have made. They also gain a sense of accomplishment from helping other women see that change is possible and from helping other women work on solutions of their own.

Services for Children

Children's programs are an important part of the services provided at shelters for battered women. Most of the women who stay at a shelter bring their children with them if possible. Living with battering in the home affects each child differently. For example, some children become fearful and withdrawn. Others become hostile and aggressive. Shelters try to provide a safe, welcoming environment for all children during their stay. No physical punishment is allowed at the shelter. Free child care is provided so that women can attend counseling sessions, informational workshops, support group meetings, and have some time to themselves. However, the women themselves are still expected to be their children's primary caretaker during the shelter stay.

Many shelters have small budgets and not enough volunteers, so they are not able to offer very extensive programs for children. They all try to provide some kind of recreational activities, and some sort of initial orientation to help the children understand why they are there and what to expect. Where shelters do not have a professional child psychologist or therapist on staff, they can refer you to someone suitable. If you have any questions about how your children are being affected by violence in the home and what you can do to help them, you can raise these concerns with shelter staff.

Educational Workshops
and Written Material

Many shelters for battered women provide educational workshops on topics that would be of particular interest to battered women. For example, such workshops might cover: money management; parenting; how the legal system operates in cases of domestic assault; how to deal with stress; job hunting; nutrition; or, coping with divorce. Workshops may be offered by shelter staff or cosponsored with other community agencies. Even if you are not staying at the shelter you can participate in educational workshops. Shelter staff can tell you what kinds of workshops are already being offered, when, and where. If there is a topic missing, in which you are especially interested, speak up and suggest it. Other women probably share your interest. The shelter may be able to set up a session devoted to this topic or suggest another way you can find the training you want.

Shelters also prepare and distribute written materials informing battered women and the general public about the nature and extent of woman battering and the kinds of services available to help battered women. Much of this material is available free of charge or at very low cost. If the nearest shelter is too far away for you to get there easily, ask to have some of the printed material they have available mailed to you. Have it sent to you somewhere other than your home address if you are worried about your husband or boyfriend finding it. The information shelter staff can provide about the general dynamics of battering is useful to battered women themselves, and to anyone who has an interest in someone who is being battered. Contacting a shelter is a good way to learn more about battering.

Advocacy

In addition to listening and providing information, shelter staff are there to be your advocates. Advocacy means active support. For example, shelter volunteers may be able to go with you to court; to the hospital; to your child's school; to apply for a loan or for welfare benefits; or to your home if you go back to collect your things. They will help you fill out necessary forms, help you arrange transportation and child care, help you make the right contacts, and argue on your behalf if you are not being treated fairly. Advocacy means you are not alone; you have people behind you. When shelter staff actively stand up for battered women there is a better chance that your needs will be taken seriously.

Advocacy extends to community education. Speakers representing domestic assault/family violence programs give talks at schools, churches, clubs, and other organizations to make people more aware of the problems battered women have and more understanding of what is involved for victims. Shelter staff are also active in efforts to train personnel at other agencies — police officers, prosecuting attorneys, counselors in mental health clinics, hospital staff, social workers, etc. — to better handle cases involving battering. They lobby for changes in the law and in agency policies that would be beneficial for battered women.

Advice and Referral

Information about resources available in the community to assist battered women and appropriate referrals can be readily obtained from a shelter for battered women. Shelter staff can answer many of the questions you may have, and suggest other individuals or agencies to contact for further assistance. For example, if you leave your partner, what kinds of help can you get from local social service agencies? If you are injured, how can you get to the hospital? Do you need a lawyer? If so, how do you find one? If you call the police, will they arrest the batterer even if he does not do anything to you while they are there? If you have him arrested, what will happen to him? Will you have to go to court? Is there any other way to get him to stay away from you or stop battering? Is there a batterers' counseling program for him in your community? What kind of help can you get from the shelter itself? Can you call any time, day or night? How long can you stay? Can you stay more than once? What does it cost? Can you bring children? Is there a waiting list? And so on. The advantage of contacting a shelter for battered women is that staff members already have at hand all kinds of information and suggestions that are certain to be of use to you. They will be able to save you a considerable amount of time, energy, and frustration. Even if there is no domestic assault/family violence program located in your immediate community, call the nearest shelter for battered women and see what advice they have to offer.

Finding a Shelter In or Near Your Community

The first step in contacting a shelter for battered women is to look in the telephone book or call telephone information for the number of the battered women's shelter or domestic assault/family violence program in or nearest to your own community. Look at the beginning pages of your local

telephone directory for Community Service Numbers or under the heading "Abuse and Assault" in the yellow pages.
You can also call local information (dial 1-555-1212) and
ask the operator for the number of a "crisis line" or "help
line" to call about problems with domestic assault or family
violence.

There are domestic violence programs all over the coun-
try but each one is a little different. You will have to find
out more about what kinds of help you can get in your area.
If you have trouble finding out what number to call, if the
line is busy, or you do not like the first person you talk to;
do not give up. Do not be discouraged. Keep trying! If you
feel suspicious or mistrustful, ashamed or embarrassed,
nervous or scared, that is not unusual. Allow yourself to
have these feelings, but do not let them stop you from getting the help you want and need.

Call and talk to someone now! Do not wait for an emergency. Remember the cycle of violence? After an episode
of battering is over the tendency is to convince yourself that
everything is okay and that it will never happen again. But
what if . . . ? Wouldn't you feel more secure if you knew
exactly what kind of outside support is available to you?
Find out now. If you have ever been battered, in any way,
you have a right to know. Remember, you are not commit-
ting yourself to anything; you are just getting information.

When it comes to taking action, simply getting information may not seem like a big accomplishment, but it is an
important example of how you can make a plan and carry it
out. It is an example of one step you can take to make
changes in your life.

7
Medical Care and
Psychological counseling

Not all communities have an established shelter for
battered women or a domestic assault program. However, in
every community there are professionals in health and
human services (such as doctors, nurses, social workers, or
psychologists) who may be able to help you. One drawback
is that not all health and human service professionals have
special knowledge of woman battering. A lack of
understanding of the nature of domestic assault will affect
the way professionals respond to you. Knowing their
possible limitations in meeting your needs will help you
make better use of the services they can provide.

Going to the Doctor
Severe physical injuries and chronic health problems
bring many battered women into contact with medical prac-
titioners. Yet most of the beatings battered women receive
will not come to a doctor's attention. How many times have
you been physically battered and not gone for professional

medical care? For minor scrapes and bruises it may not have been worth the time, bother, and expense to you. What about more serious injuries? Do you find yourself waiting to see a doctor until you are forced to go because of severe bodily harm?

There are good reasons to get medical care:

1. You deserve the attention! When someone is attacked by a stranger, they do not hesitate to get needed medical care. If you are physically assaulted by your husband or lover, you have the same right to receive professional medical treatment. This may be hard to remember or believe when the batterer belittles your pain and bullies you, threatens you, or tries to physically restrain you from going to the doctor or to a hospital. This is one of the situations in which a neighbor, relative, or friend can be supportive — giving encouragement and practical assistance in getting you to the doctor's office or a hospital emergency room.

    Sometimes, not seeing a doctor comes down to how you feel about yourself and your future. One battered woman explained, "It didn't seem worth the trouble to go get fixed up . . . for what? So he could start beating me all over again and do the same or worse." Then why bother to get medical attention? Because it is one of those actions you can take that help you maintain your own sense of caring and respect for yourself, regardless of how he treats you. Do not leave it up to the batterer to decide whether or not you need medical care. Even if you have to sneak away to do it, get yourself taken care of as best you can.

2. Medical records help to document the abuse you have
    experienced. If your partner goes for counseling, your
    medical records can be useful in confronting him with
    the actual consequences of his behavior, which he is
    likely to deny. If you decide, later, to take legal action
    against him, medical records will help make your case
    stronger. Your will have supporting evidence that his
    abusive behavior has not been limited to one incident
    and that it is therefore likely to be repeated. Since a lot
    of battering goes on in the privacy of the home, where
    it is not directly witnessed by other adults, medical
    records might be the most accurate available reflection
    of the nature and extent of battering, outside of your
    own testimony.

Get medical help for your injuries, and when you talk to
the doctor do not minimize what is wrong. Let the doctor
know exactly where you hurt, how much, and for how long.
You do not have to tell exactly how you got hurt if you do
not want to. That is up to you.

Confiding in the Doctor

As a battered woman, seeking medical care involves
more than simply attending to the physical injuries themselves. You are always faced with the question of whether
or not to reveal the source of your injuries. Consider, first,
that nobody can make you tell. You can decide to confide
in your doctor or you can decide not to. If the doctor asks
how you were hurt, you can make up a story even if it does
not sound very convincing. You also have the option to say

nothing, or to say that you really do not want to talk about it at this time.*

Doctors typically are not trained to encourage you to talk about emotional issues. They have many patients and limited time for consultation. They see their primary task as healing the body, not dealing with social problems. Outside of a medical degree, they usually have no special expertise or knowledge for treating cases of spouse abuse. Most doctors will not be inclined to pursue the subject, especially if you object.

On the other hand, you might decide you want to confide in your doctor. In this case, if you just hint around and hope the doctor will guess or take time out to coax it out of you, you might be disappointed. Try telling the facts in as straightforward a manner as you can manage. If the doctor asks, "How did this happen?", take the opportunity to say, "My husband and I had a fight," and explain exactly what your partner did that caused your injury. If you do not want anyone else — including your partner — to know what you have told the doctor, say so. Insist that what you have said must be kept confidential. For more generalized, chronic health problems that are a result of being in an abusive relationship — insomnia, fatigue, tension headaches, colitis, and so on — there is even less chance that the doctor will guess exactly what is going on. You will have to speak up and tell the doctor about the circumstances at home that are upsetting you if you want the doctor to know.

If you find it difficult to bring the subject of battering up with your doctor initially, you might try talking to one of

---

*Do keep in mind that the more details you can provide about how the injuries occurred — even if you do not go so far as to say, "My husband did this to me" — the better able the doctor will be to treat you.

the nurses first. If you get the feeling that your doctor is putting you off or deliberately ignoring your attempts to discuss the source of your specific injuries and general distress, consider looking for another doctor who is more responsive. Individual doctors have their own personal styles of consultation. If you want to talk openly about the battering, you need a doctor who is willing to listen.

It is unrealistic, though, to expect a doctor to give you detailed advice concerning what to do about the battering relationship. The advice you get, if any is offered, will mainly reflect the personal inclinations and beliefs of the individual doctor concerned. The opinions expressed may be helpful and supportive, or they may not. Based on the kind of reaction you get, you can decide whether this is someone you want to keep talking to about your home situation or whether you will go to the doctor simply for medical care and seek advice elsewhere.

If you go back to the same doctor for treatment after future battering incidents, do not be surprised if the doctor shows some impatience with you. Many doctors, genuinely concerned with their patients' physical well-being, do not understand why a woman would stay with a battering man. To an outsider, leaving seems like a simple solution. If you think it might help, try to explain your reasons for staying. Emphasize that you are doing the best you can right now and that the doctor's continued care and support are important to you. If the doctor is still unsympathetic and cannot respect your decision, consider looking for a new doctor.

Use of Medication

Another problem area is the role of the doctor in prescribing medication for the emotional upset experienced by battered women. If you complain of feeling nervous, tense, anxious, or "on edge," a doctor is likely to prescribe drugs — tranquilizers, for example. You may feel too that medication will help you cope with the strain you are under. Be cautious about using drugs. Keep in mind that they are only treating the symptoms of an abusive relationship, not the cause of your physical and emotional distress. Battering is the cause. The doctor is only treating the damage done to you, not the battering itself.

If you want medication to calm your nerves or ease your pain, do go to the doctor. When you are taking drugs, periodically ask yourself the following kinds of questions: Is the doctor prescribing drugs without confronting the underlying problem of battering? Is the medication you are taking helping you to calm down so you can think more clearly about what to do? Are you remaining alert and able to respond in an emergency? Or, are you feeling drowsy and detached from what is going on around you? Along with the pain and nervousness, have you lost your motivation to change the relationship itself and do something about the battering? Is the medication a short-term measure to get you through a crisis or is it more and more becoming a crutch that maintains the battering relationship? Taking drugs recommended by the doctor to help you get by is okay as long as you are honest with yourself about the reasons and remain critical about the long-term effect.

The Hospital as a Resource

Doctors and other health professionals can do a great deal to help ease a battered woman's physical pain. Contact with health professionals can also help the battered woman overcome her sense of isolation. Emergency rooms in hospitals are accessible 24 hours a day, seven days a week. Despite the waiting and red tape, the hospital can be a good place to go for help. If you need to go to a hospital as a result of a battering incident you will probably have a sense of urgency about the danger you are in from your partner. While you are there it may be possible for you to find out more about community services available to battered women. Ask if you can talk to a hospital social worker. See what information hospital staff can give you about the nearest shelter for battered women or a local crisis line you can call. If the battering man has gone with you to the emergency room, make an excuse — like going to the bathroom or to get a drink of water — to be away from him long enough to speak to someone at the information desk privately. If you are in too much pain or confusion right after a beating to take such steps, just keep the hospital in mind as a place where you can find out about other kinds of help available in your community.

Going to a Professional Counselor

As discussed in Chapter 1, battering has emotional as well as physical effects. Battered women often experience feelings such as anger, confusion, panic, hopelessness, self-hate, insecurity, and despair that undermine their sense of well-being and their ability to function. They have difficulty sorting out and understanding the complex mix of positive and negative feelings they have about their relationship with the battering man. How can you love or need a man who is abusive to you? Yet you do. How can you fear or hate a man whose life is so much a part of your own? Yet you do. Talking to neighbors, family, and friends can help, but sometimes a professional counselor can also be a valuable resource. Professional counselors are persons whose job is to "counsel" or advise others. They have had some kind of special training in counseling methods and practical experience helping people with a variety of personal and family problems. Professionals from whom you might seek counsel include psychiatrists (medical doctors with a specialization in mental disorders), psychologists, family counselors, social workers, or church leaders (minister, priest, or rabbi).

Consider the following possible advantages of talking to a professional counselor:

- sometimes it is easier to talk to someone who is not so close to you emotionally;

- what you tell a professional counselor is confidential; no one else will know;

- professional counselors are trained to be attentive listeners, and to encourage you to talk about yourself — your experiences, thoughts, and feelings;

- professional counselors can be more systematic and objective than neighbors, relatives, or friends in looking at the problems you are facing;

- professionals counselors know a variety of exercises and techniques that can help you clarify your thoughts and feelings, express yourself more easily, and make changes you want to make in your behavior.

Individual counselors vary in their approach, depending on their training, type of practice, and personality. To help you, a counselor must be someone you can respect and trust. This does not mean it will be easy. Facing feelings we have been hiding from ourselves, revealing secrets we have felt ashamed to tell anyone, confronting our own conflicting thoughts and desires about the battering man and our relationship with him can be a painful process. A counselor who is right for you can guide and encourage you so that you come away knowing more about yourself, feeling stronger and better able to take care of yourself.

Finding the Right Counselor for You

There are several ways to locate professional counselors. Ask people you know personally if they can recommend someone. For instance, have they ever talked to a minister or a psychologist about a family program? Did it help? You can call the nearest shelter for battered women and ask if they can recommend people outside their own staff who would be good. Call the Department of Social Services or a local community center and ask whether there is a social worker you could talk to about family problems such as spouse abuse. Check the *Yellow Pages* in your local telephone directory under the following headings: "Counseling," "Physicians & Surgeons — Psychiatry," "Social Service Organizations," "Marriage & Family Counselors," "Psychologists," "Social Workers." Make some initial phone calls. Ask how much they charge for their services. Ask them to give you some idea what general approach they take in counseling and what kinds of problems they deal with most often. Ask if they have any experience dealing specifically with cases of spouse abuse/woman battering/domestic assault, and how they would try to help women in this situation. If you are encouraged by the counselor's attitude and style of communicating, ask if you can make a brief, low-cost first visit to meet the counselor in person and discuss what you might be able to get out of a period of professional counseling. Make a specific appointment and get the details you need about when, where, and how to get there.

The first visit may be awkward, but remember you have not committed yourself to anything, you are just trying to find out what this particular person might have to offer. Before you go, sit down and think about what it is you are hoping to gain from counseling. List some of the questions that are on your mind. Write all this down, and bring it with you. If you get nervous and forget what you wanted to say, you can refer to what you have written. You can even let the counselor read some of what you have written and see how he or she responds to the concerns you have expressed.

Do not be surprised if you find yourself "losing control" (getting very emotional) as you begin talking about your reasons for seeking counseling. If you are embarrassed, remember that finding a safe and supportive setting where you can let all this out is one of the reasons you are there. A professional counselor is prepared to handle this, and should be able to reassure you that your behavior is not unusual.

You need to find a counselor who knows enough to accept that what you are telling him or her about the battering is true and who will put your safety first, not assume that the relationship with your partner is more important to protect. A counselor should also be able to recognize and nurture the strengths you have that will help you come to terms with the problems you are facing.

Involving the Batterer in Counseling

Up to this point we have been considering individual psychological counseling for the woman who has been battered. Such counseling can be very useful in helping you sort out your own feelings and conflicts so that you can better decide what you want for yourself. Its major limitation is that *individual psychological counseling for you does not stop your partner's abusive behavior.* For the battering to end, your partner needs to change. He needs help sorting out his feelings and conflicts and find non-violent ways to deal with them. Ideally, he should realize this and seek help on his own. By now you know that batterers rarely do. Still, your partner is an individual, not a statistic. If you think he might be persuaded to get help, here is what you can do.

Use the same methods suggested earlier to see if you can locate one or more counselors who might be able to work with you and your partner as a couple or counsel him, individually or as part of a group. Check these people out yourself first. See if you feel you can trust the kind of advice they would give your partner. Ask how much experience they have had in counseling men who batter. Ask them questions about woman battering; what they think causes it and what they think should be done about it. Ask about their goals in counseling battering men or couples in which the man is abusive. Then make a list of the names and addresses of the counselors you would trust to work with your husband or boyfriend. Give this list to your partner. Tell him you want him to go for help and outline the advantages. For instance, he should get help now to learn other, non-abusive ways of handling conflicts before he hurts you more than he ever expected, before violence destroys your relationship, before he is arrested by the police for domestic assault. If you think it is appropriate, ask anyone you know who might be able to convince him — a mutual friend, teacher, relative, neighbor, family doctor or lawyer — to encourage him to go for help. If you are separated from him because of abuse, make his seeking help and staying with it a condition of your return.

Ending violence in the relationship must be the immediate, explicit, and primary purpose of any counseling that involves your partner. No substitute is acceptable. This may sound extreme, but there are good reasons behind it. If ending violence in the relationship is *not* the counselor's foremost goal:

- Counseling may get sidetracked dealing with other problems the battering man has. While this may be beneficial for your partner, it will not necessarily stop the battering.

- The counselor may fail to effectively confront the batterer and overcome his denial. The batterer will remain resistant to change.

- Worse, a counselor who accepts the batterer's justifications at face value may unintentionally encourage your partner's abusive behavior and "blaming the victim" mentality.

- Counseling that proceeds with the primary goal of keeping a couple together is not in your best interests. If the battering does not stop first, keeping the couple together means promoting an abusive relationship.

- Counseling may raise stressful, threatening issues for your partner before he has developed non-abusive ways of handling such stress. Conflicts that arise in counseling may then spill over into violence at home.

As cautioned in Chapter 3, counseling for your partner may not work, but at least it is directed at the battering man himself, not just his victim. If your partner refuses to participate in counseling at all or if you see that counseling will be ineffective in ending the battering, you have one more reason not to feel guilty about whatever actions you take to protect yourself. You will have given him every opportunity to stop battering.

8
The Legal System

No matter how much the battering man tries to minimize or justify his use of physical force in the home he is in fact violating the law when he assaults you. Domestic assault is a crime. The battering man can be arrested and prosecuted. Most instances of domestic assault still do not result in criminal charges. Yet police, prosecuting attorneys, and the courts are increasingly willing to cooperate in efforts to prosecute a battering spouse.

Deciding to Press Charges
In an earlier chapter, it was noted that battering men often have the idea that their behavior should not have negative consequences. They may feel that they have a right to use physical force at home without outside interference. Even when they are remorseful about the first incidents of battering, over time they seem to rationalize their behavior. It is common for battered women to report that after the first time her partner hit her it seemed to become easier for him to hit her again. This may be, in part, because the lack of effective social intervention in cases of battering means

the batterer finds he can "get away with it." Pressing criminal charges is one way of trying to convey to the battering man that his actions are not acceptable and can result in negative consequences for him.

Most battered women have mixed feelings about pursuing criminal prosecution against a spouse. They tend to use this option only as a last resort. However, a study in Minneapolis showed that of three standard police responses to nonlife-threatening domestic violence calls (arrest, attempting to counsel both parties, or sending the assailant away from home for several hours) arrest showed the lowest incidence of repeated violence within a six-month follow-up period. Thus, it is worth considering the possibility of arrest as one measure to try to reduce future incidents of physical assault. Additionally, in potentially life-threatening situations, arrest may be the best way to protect yourself and gain some time to seek refuge.

Steps in Prosecution for Domestic Assault

The legal system is complex in structure, confusing in its operation, and often disappointing in the results you will get, but it is one of the resources available to you as a battered woman. The more you know about how it works, the better you will be able to decide whether this is an option you want to pursue. The chart which follows will help you visualize the steps involved in pressing charges for domestic assault. These steps are discussed in more detail in Appendix G. You begin by filing a complaint with the police or sheriff's department. Their report is reviewed by the prosecuting attorney's office. If your complaint is authorized by the prosecuting attorney's office you sign it in the presence of a judge. After the judge signs your complaint an arrest warrant is issued. The police take some action on the warrant to bring your assailant to court. He appears in court to hear the official charges against him. If he pleads guilty, the judge determines what penalty ("sentence") is appropriate. If your assailant pleads not guilty a trial is scheduled.

What You Should Know about the Legal System

If you are thinking of pressing charges against your battering partner, the following features of the criminal justice system will be important to consider.

The criminal justice system's primary role is law enforcement. Police, prosecuting attorneys, and judges are not like social workers or counseling psychologists who are trained to focus on your emotional needs. The main job of persons in the criminal justice system is to enforce the law. In their contacts with you they will be trying to gather information pertaining to the legal aspects of the battering situation. Their questions may seem blunt and insensitive, difficult and embarrassing, even offensive at times. For example, you will have to describe the circumstances of the assault repeatedly. You may be asked to give details about your relationship with the assailant that seem very personal. Police officers and prosecuting attorneys may be skeptical about your willingness to follow through on a complaint or may try to discourage you from pressing charges.

Some of the procedures that help build a stronger legal case against an assailant are not easy for the victim. For example, pictures taken of your cuts and bruises can be used to document the injuries sustained as a result of an assault. Having such pictures taken may come as an unexpected embarrassment. If you decide to press charges, it helps to have outside support — someone who can go with you at various stages of the criminal justice process and someone with whom you can discuss your feelings about it. Friends, relatives, neighbors, and professional counselors can help. Advocates from a shelter for battered women or some other type of victim assistance program can also guide you and speak up on your behalf.

Law enforcement procedures vary. Laws pertaining to domestic assault differ from state to state and law enforcement procedures vary greatly, even from one community to the next. Find out how domestic assault cases are handled in your community. Call the general information number listed in the telephone directory for each agency — the police or sheriff's department, the prosecuting attorney's office, the courts — and ask to talk to someone who is familiar with how the agency operates in cases of domestic assault. You do not have to identify yourself as a battered woman. These are public service agencies and any community member has a right to request such information. To save time you might first check with the nearest shelter for battered women and see what information they already have available.

Get a general idea of how the system works as a whole. For details, ask more specific questions, such as: Can a police officer arrest without a warrant for misdemeanor assault in cases of domestic violence (on "probable cause") even if the man does not do anything to her while the police are present? Are domestic assault cases identified and treated differently than other types of assault? How seriously are they taken? How supportive of victims are police, prosecuting attorneys, and judges? On what basis does the prosecuting attorney's office decide whether or not to authorize a domestic assault complaint? What kinds of sentences are usually given in cases of misdemeanor domestic assault? How can a victim find out when an arraignment will be scheduled? Can she be present at the pre-sentence conference? How much weight will be given to her statement? And so on.

It will be up to you to keep informed about the progress of your case. In the process of pressing charges there are many steps along the way at which a case can be closed, delayed, or resolved. Moreover, the different agencies involved in the criminal justice system tend to operate independently of one another to a considerable extent. This means that it is often difficult to find out what is happening with your case. You will not automatically be kept informed. The case might be settled, or dismissed, without you even knowing.

Be *active* in following the case, be *persistent,* and *use advocates* to help you. The chart, "Steps in Prosecution of Domestic Assault," which is provided in this chapter (modified or supplemented by what you learn about law enforcement procedures in your own community) can serve as a guide. Write down the names and phone numbers of each of the persons with whom you have contact along the way. At each step, ask:

1. What happens next?

2. How long will it take?

3. Who, specifically, should I contact to find out how the case is progressing?

Steps in Prosecution
for Domestic Assault*

Use this chart to compare with procedures followed in your own community. (See also Appendix G.)

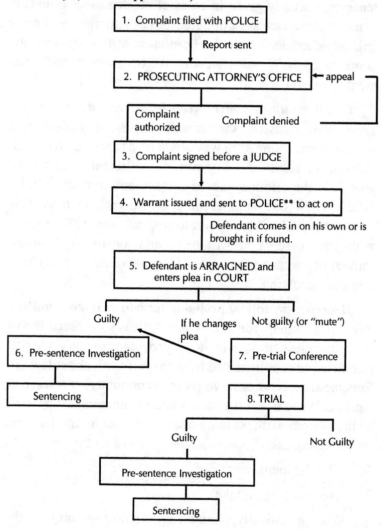

---

*From a chart developed by the YWCA Domestic Assault Program in Kalamazoo, MI.
**Or other law enforcement agency.

You have the right to ask for explanations. If you get to a stage where you feel you are being ignored, or meeting with resistance, or just losing track, go back to someone who was helpful earlier and ask that person to call for you to find out the status of your case. Callers who represent another law enforcement or social-service agency may get a better reception than an individual caller. They are also more likely to have established relationships with staff at other agencies and to know whom to contact for different kinds of information.

You will need to know what is happening with your assailant, when he will be in custody and when he will be released. It is particularly important for you to know when the case is reaching a step where you may have an opportunity to influence the decisions being made. You want the court to be mindful of your safety and to take your wishes into account whenever possible. Advocates can help you represent your interests more forcefully and help keep you informed about your case.

Your assailant will probably remain at liberty. Following the principle that a person charged with a crime is "innocent until proven guilty," our legal system provides for the accused to remain at liberty until actually convicted and sentenced to serve time in jail or prison. Before trial, your partner is likely to be released on his promise to appear in court when his case is to be heard. He may also be required to pay a sum of money (his "bail") as determined by the court to guarantee his appearance. If you rely on the battering man for economic support, this procedure has the advantage of minimizing his time away from work, though the bail requirement may sometimes be a hardship. However, if he is angry and determined to punish you, his release puts you at risk of further abuse.

If your assailant is arrested right after a battering incident and taken to jail, find out how long he will be held in custody. Law enforcement officers sensitive to the unique problems involved in domestic assault cases may try to keep the battering man in custody at least overnight to give the victim time to either get her things together and move to a safe location, or to initiate a complaint and be interviewed by the prosecuting attorney's office without harassment from her partner. When a complaint is filed, the man can be held in custody a day or two until arraignment if it is believed he will otherwise commit another assault. However, routinely he will be released. Also, if he was not arrested at the time of the assault, he will be at liberty until he appears in court for arraignment. You might even be living together while waiting for him to be notified, with all the uncertainty that involves for you about how he will react. After arraignment, pending sentencing he will again be out on bail in most cases.

Having Second Thoughts

The longest period of waiting and the greatest stress for victims of domestic assault usually occurs if the batterer pleads not guilty and is out on bail until his trial. This is when many battered women seek to have charges against their assailant dropped. As time goes by they have second thoughts. Sometimes they give in to feelings of *guilt*. The man who batters you may try to persuade you that if you still love him or care about his children you should not pursue criminal charges. He may say things like, "Please don't do this to me"; "It is your fault this is happening"; or, "We can still work things out." Keep in mind that you have already given him many, many second chances; that he has brought prosecution on himself by his own actions in violation of the law, and; that what is happening to him may not turn out to be such a bad thing if he finally quits battering.

The batterer's threats are another kind of problem. Battered women are often criticized for failing to follow through on a complaint but less attention is given to the fact that they are frequently subjected to repeated *threats* from their assailant, with whom they may not be able to avoid contact during the time he is waiting for trial. Police and prosecuting attorneys may, understandably, be annoyed with complainants who want to drop charges after considerable time, effort, and expense have gone into bringing a case to court. However, they are not with you or the people close to you 24 hours a day to provide protection from the batterer who may decide to carry out his threats. It is little comfort to be told that you can call for help again after something bad happens, or that many batterers do not carry out their threats. What is he threatening to do? How likely is it that he will actually do what he says? What steps can you take to protect yourself?

When you initiate your complaint with the police and when you are interviewed at the prosecuting attorney's office, discuss any concerns you have about your safety if you press charges. Get as much information as you can about how your particular case is going to be handled so that you are not caught by surprise when the batterer is released. After you sign an authorized complaint in the presence of a judge and a warrant is issued, you may no longer have the power to drop charges. Dropping charges will then be left to the prosecuting attorney's office. This has the advantage of taking some pressure off you. You can honestly say to the batterer that the decision to drop changes is no longer yours to make.

The batterer may plead guilty at arraignment. If you are having second thoughts at this time, you might make a pre-sentence statement requesting mandatory counseling or other terms of probation for the batterer instead of jail time. You also have some say with the prosecuting attorney's office in whether or not the case goes to trial if your assailant pleads not guilty because it will be difficult to obtain a conviction without your continued cooperation. Be cautious though about taking steps which may unintentionally confirm the batterer's idea that he can manipulate you with threats or promises in order to avoid the consequences of his behavior.

Warning Letters

In limited situations the use of a "warning letter" instead of arrest and prosecution is possible. When a misdemeanor violation is involved and there is sufficient evidence in the case to prosecute but the assailant appears to be an otherwise law-abiding citizen (without criminal record), you may request that the prosecuting attorney's office send him a warning letter. Warning letters may be used, for example, when your partner's behavior indicates ignorance or misunderstanding of the law; when he does not believe that his actions toward you are really criminal. The letter outlines the nature of the charge which has been brought against him and expresses the hope that a warning is sufficient for such behavior to cease. An example of a warning letter is provided in Appendix G. Once the alternative of a warning letter is chosen, though, you may not be able to obtain a criminal warrant for the original offense if your partner's reaction is not favorable. However, you can file a new complaint if another battering incident occurs. Try to obtain a warning letter from the prosecuting attorney's office if you do not yet want to press charges but do want to impress on your partner your determination to take whatever steps are necessary to stop the battering.

Please see Appendix G for further guidelines for when you speak with a prosecutor or an attorney, and Appendix H when appearing in court.

Victim Assistance Programs

Some communities have a victim-assistance program connected with the prosecuting attorney's office. This is a resource which is frequently overlooked by victims of domestic assault. Through a victim-assistance program you may be able to apply for money from a victim compensation fund. This fund is used to help reduce the financial losses of victims who have suffered physical or emotional injury from violent crime. For example, compensation funds might cover your hospital expenses, lost wages, or the cost of psychological counseling. In addition, victim assistance programs offer services such as answering any questions you might have about the criminal justice system, going with you for court appearances, helping you prepare a pre-sentence statement for the judge, and keeping you informed about the progress of your case. To qualify for victim assistance you must make an official complaint against the batterer and be willing to cooperate with law enforcement officials if prosecution is authorized.

Injunctive (or Restraining) Orders

In theory, injunctive orders can be used to prevent, or "restrain," your partner from threatening, molesting, assaulting, or beating you without bringing criminal changes against him. If your husband or ex-husband, lover or ex-lover has threatened or actually harmed you, a judge can issue a court order telling him to stop. To obtain an injunctive order there are forms that will need to be filled out and submitted to the appropriate court. Your petition for a court order will have to convince a judge to give you the court's protection. In your petition give as much detail as you can about what has happened:

- when the incident took place; day and time,

- where it took place,

- what was said to frighten you and what was done to hurt you,

- whether or not there were children present and what happened to them,

- whether or not there were any other witnesses who saw what happened,

- if the police came, what they did,

- whether or not you or the children went to a doctor, clinic, or hospital for treatment afterwards, and

- how many times you have been threatened or hurt before.

Let the court know that your situation is serious and that if you do not get help right away you and your children will be in danger. If you have kept records of previous abuse, use them as a guide in preparing your statement. You may also need a lawyer to help you in preparing and filing a request for an injunctive or restraining order. Check on the procedures followed in your district. A sample injunctive order appears in Appendix G.

An injunctive or restraining order does not go into effect until it is personally delivered to ("served" on) the abuser. It will then be in effect only for the limited amount of time specified by the order. Police are empowered to enforce an injunctive or restraining order once it is properly filed with them, but *no action can be taken until the abuser is in violation of the order.* When the police are called in they can arrest if they are able to confirm the existence of a valid order which has been properly served and can determine that one or more of the prohibited actions specified on the order has been violated. Examine the wording of the injunctive order closely so you know what these actions are. Police are sometimes reluctant to enforce such orders because officers are liable for false arrest if the order has been misfiled, changed, or rescinded. You should keep a copy of the order with you and be aware of its expiration date. You might also check with your local police or sheriff's department to be sure they have an official copy on file.

There are legal penalties for violation of an injunctive or restraining order. A person who violates the terms of a court order is subject to criminal contempt of court charges and if found guilty by a judge can be given fines of up to $500 and/or jail up to 90 days. You might try an injunctive or restraining order if you do not want to press criminal

charges but do want to take some kind of legal action to let
the batterer know that you are serious about trying to stop
his abuse. Court injunctions may be effective as a preventa-
tive measure if your partner basically respects the authority
of the court or wants to avoid the possibility of being arrested for violating the order. Injunctive orders are sometimes sought in connection with a divorce action, after a
couple has separated, to try to keep the battering man away
from a woman's residence and prevent him from violating
custody and visitation orders. Again, the injunctive order is
only as effective in preventing abuse as the batterer's willingness to comply. This you can best determine from your
own experience with him.

Seeking Legal Counsel

There are other legal actions you can take. These are
handled through private attorneys or the Legal Aid Bureau.
You might start by contacting the nearest shelter for battered women to ask for a legal referral or call your local
county bar association's lawyer referral service and ask for
the names of several attorneys with experience in handling
cases involving domestic assault. Private attorneys and the
Legal Aid Bureau will also be listed in the yellow pages of
your telephone directory. In selecting an attorney look for
an individual who is knowledgeable and experienced in the
type of legal action you want to take and who has some understanding of the unique problems involved for women
who are victims of battering.

Ask for a brief initial interview during which you can
describe the basics of your situation and get the lawyer's
suggestions for possible actions you can take. Writing down

some of your questions beforehand might be helpful. Take notes too when you talk to the lawyer if you are concerned about forgetting an important point. Ask for explanations to be given in everyday language you can understand. If you want a friend or advocate to go with you to see the lawyer, bring them along.

In seeking legal advice, request opinions from several lawyers and focus on what alternatives are available. Some attorneys will provide free half-hour initial consultations; other may be able and willing to give you some general beginning information over the phone. Ask about their fees and, if money is a problem, discuss possible financial arrangements that might be made, including having your spouse pay some of the attorney's fees. If you feel you cannot afford a private attorney, check with the Legal Aid Bureau. They have lawyers who may be able to represent you at no cost to you or for a reduced fee. In either case, you need to find a lawyer who you are confident will do a good job of representing your interests.

Evaluating Your Legal Options

The legal system provides both criminal and civil options for women who are victimized by battering. Recently, more attention has been given to arrest as an effective police response in lowering repeated incidents of domestic assault. In deciding whether or not to press criminal charges you will have to consider the circumstances in your case. What is it you want to accomplish by pressing charges? Would a warning letter be sufficient? Is the batterer an individual who may be shocked enough by confrontation with the reality of criminal prosecution to change his behavior?

Or, is he already extremely violent and angry so that criminal prosecution will be effective only if it results in his imprisonment? What will happen if you press charges but he is not convicted? How safe will you be while the case is being taken to court? How fearful are you of his threats? If you are considering dropping charges, will you really be any safer in the long run if you do not press charges? Or, will the batterer simply continue to feel that he can get away with doing whatever he wants? How many cases do you know of in which the batterer was so "grateful" for his victim's withdrawing a complaint that he never hit her again? Will you feel better about yourself if you do press charges, or if you do not?

Obtaining an injunctive or restraining order is a civil court proceeding. It is another way to let the batterer know that you are going to take some legal action against him even if you are not willing to pursue criminal charges. Civil court orders do carry possible (but minor) criminal penalties for violation. Legal separation and divorce are also civil actions you can take. Be sure to consult a lawyer who can explain the legal issues involved in everyday language. Look for someone who is knowledgeable and understanding about woman battering, and who you feel can successfully represent your interests in court. Find out what your legal options are, weigh the pros and cons of each, and do what makes the most sense to you. Keep in mind that you are likely to have conflicting feelings about whatever legal action you decide to take. This does not mean you have made the wrong decision. If you are confused about what actions to take or are feeling very unsure of yourself, counseling may help. Staff at the nearest shelter or program for battered women can be particularly helpful in providing information and emotional support.

9
To Stay or Not to Stay

If you are a battered woman you have probably spent a lot of time trying to figure out what to do. You probably still have mixed feelings. Most women do not want to just walk out on a relationship that is important to them. Maybe you tried leaving before but then went back because it was so hard to get by on your own or because you still cared about him and he promised to change. If, in your case, there are still some good times at home or if there are some particularly strong reasons for "sticking it out," you may wonder how someone finally decides to leave a battering man.

Shelter workers know that women stay in battering relationships for many different reasons:

- hope that her partner will change and the battering will end,

- fear of what the batterer will do if she tries to leave,

- awareness of the serious practical difficulties she will face in trying to make it on her own,

- lack of confidence in herself,
- emotional ties to the battering man,
- social pressures to stay even if she does not love him anymore.

For many such reasons and her own belief in the importance of having a man and being a good partner to him, a battered woman may make extraordinary efforts to placate and accommodate the batterer so as to keep their relationship together. The conviction that she "belongs" with this man, and has no choice but to stay, motivates her to keep working on the relationship rather than leave it. For a woman to leave an abusive relationship she must at some point begin to question her basic assumptions, loyalties, and priorities. She may have to re-evaluate many traditional attitudes and beliefs about her identity as a woman as well as her commitment to this particular man. What are the limits of self-sacrifice in a relationship? Does a man who is abusive have a right to my continued commitment? Is it really "selfish" to want a life for myself and my children free of the threat of violence? Why should his needs be considered more important than mine? Is this the only man I could ever love? Is being with a man so important that you have to stay no matter what the costs? Can the alternatives really be worse? How will I know if I do not try them for myself? Leaving may seem like admitting failure, but will I ever feel good about myself if I stay?

As the battering in your relationship goes on over time you may come to realize that nothing you can do within the relationship will stop the battering. You may be forced to admit to yourself that he is not changing. You may find you are no longer able to believe his promises of reform. Staying in the relationship means that you will continue to be subjected to your partner's abusive behavior. What you get out of the relationship may no longer be enough to make up for the betrayal of trust, the constant stress, and the growing fear of increasing violence. You may finally stop believing that you have to stay no matter what the costs. Maybe for the first time he seriously threatens or injures a child in the home. Maybe you find yourself thinking of killing him if he does not kill you first. The disgust and anger you feel may come to be stronger than your desire to stay or your fear of leaving. More and more, when you look at him you see a "batterer," not a husband or lover. Though the difficulties of leaving remain great, staying with him begins to seem even more impossible. Changes like this do not happen overnight. It is easy for other people to advise you to leave and to become impatient with you if you stay. It is also easy for them to overlook or underestimate how difficult leaving can be. The obstacles include both the emotional and the practical.

Emotional Ties

Every battered woman has emotional ties to her abuser. By definition, he is not a stranger; he is someone with whom she has had an intimate relationship. The specific nature of the emotional ties will vary with the individuals involved. In a general sense, though, ending a battering relationship always means giving up a dream, the dream of sharing your life with this particular man. Initially, you may have been strongly attracted to this man. He was charming and attentive; you felt special and needed; being in love was exciting. Your relationship offered a chance to establish a family of your own; a sense of accomplishment; a feeling of

connectedness. Whether you were looking for adventure
and excitement or stability and security you had some expectations of finding what you wanted together with him.
You put a lot of yourself into this relationship. Even now
there may be times when you feel sexually or emotionally
attracted to certain qualities about him. When you think of
what your relationship could be (if only he would change)
there is a longing and sometimes a hope in the face of all
the evidence against it that if you stay you can still make
things right. Dreams die hard. In some relationships the
abusive man himself literally batters this hope away, with
increasing violence.

Living on "maybes," and "what-ifs," and the prospect
that someday he might be different is an empty and unful-
filling life. With a physically battering man, it is also a dangerous life. An abusive relationship is a direct, continuing
threat to your physical health and emotional well-being. To
leave an abusive relationship, you must look at it realistically. What rewards are you actually getting out of the relationship on a day-to-day basis? How bad are the
disappointments? How much damage has already been
done? Is this a positive relationship in which you feel good
about yourself? Are you able to develop your abilities and
expand your experience with your partner's support? Imagine yourself 10 years from now. What kind of life will you
have to look back on if you stay?

Letting go of the hope that the battering relationship
will change for the better if you stay means facing a lot of
negative feelings. Sometimes we hold on to false hopes
mainly to avoid these kinds of feelings. The idea of leaving
and striking out on your own may stir up intense feelings of
loss, failure, panic, inadequacy, loneliness, hopelessness,

abandonment, worthlessness. However, *the bad feelings you experience about the idea of leaving do not necessarily mean you should stay!* Do not assume that the best or only way to deal with fears about leaving is to stay. In fact, there is no perfect or easy solution. Staying or leaving, you are bound to be pulled emotionally in opposite directions. There are risks you take in leaving as well as risks in staying. It is not unusual to feel that no matter what you do it will be a disaster. Sometimes it will seem like you are running through a maze full of blind alleys, going in circles aimlessly, always coming back to the same place . . . forced to make a choice that you do not want to make. The option you might want most — to stay and not be battered — is not open to you if the batterer cannot or will not change. You can stay and be battered or you can try to end the battering by leaving.

Sorting Out Your Feelings and Options

Sometimes it is difficult to make decisions about what course of action to take because you have so many conflicting feelings and because there is no solution that seems exactly right for you. If so, consider taking time out to do some written exercises that will help you clarify your feelings, organize your thoughts, and reflect on the possibilities open to you.* See Appendix F for sample exercises and instructions. You can do these exercises on your own or with someone else. You can write the answers down for yourself and discuss them later with a friend or professional counselor, or you can think out loud and have another person

---

*The book, *Getting Free: A Handbook for Women in Abusive Relationships,* by Ginny NiCarthy, suggests many such activities that can help you be your own counselor.

take notes for you. Getting your thoughts on paper is an important part of these exercises because seeing things written down will make them more vivid and concrete and will help you see how everything fits together.

Temporary and Permanent Separations

In many people's minds, the way "leaving" works is that a battered woman stays and takes just so much abuse, maybe gives him one last chance, then gets fed up and leaves permanently. According to this line of reasoning, the job of outside helpers, informal or professional, is to be there for the crisis period when she has made up her mind to go, to encourage the battered woman to "make the break" and never go back. Then if she goes back to the batterer she has "had her chance," and failed. If you are a battered woman who left but then went back to the batterer, you may have sensed the disapproval of others or even felt disappointed in yourself. This is another side of "blaming the victim." If a battered woman does not leave the way we think she should, some people might say that whatever happens to her is her own fault; she deserves it. (Ideally, what she "deserves," having given the batterer another chance, at some risk to herself, is that he will live up to the trust she has put in him and stop battering, or at least become significantly less abusive.)

It is misleading to think about leaving an abusive relationship as if it is an all-or-nothing, once-and-for-all decision. Battered women typically separate from their partners and reconcile a number of times before they leave permanently, if they do leave permanently. There is no one "right" decision that we should expect all battered women to make on a schedule other people determine for her. It is probably fair to say, though, that where the pattern of battering is clearly established, where it is long term and involves severe physical assault, it is understandable if everyone concerned wants to see the victim leave immediately and permanently. Even so, as a society we have to take responsibility for providing the financial and emotional support needed by battered women to accomplish this.

Considering the broad range of experiences that can be termed "battering," there will be varying circumstances in different cases. Every woman has a right to make her own decision, taking into account:

- her batterer's behavior and attitudes,
- her own feelings — about him, their relationship, and herself,
- reactions she gets from other people to whom she turns for advice and emotional support,
- practical realities — the opportunities and constraints operating at a given time.

Temporary separations sometimes avoid the more complicated problems posed by a permanent separation. Battered women have reported the following kinds of reasons for seeking temporary separation:

- immediate survival; during an attack, if you can escape, you leave to avoid further injury;

- before a physical assault, if you see signs you have learned to associate with oncoming violence, you can leave to let things cool off, to try to avoid being battered;*

- you can leave temporarily after an abusive incident as a "protest," to let your partner know that what he has done is not right, to emphasize that you do not accept his behavior;

- you can leave to try to show him how difficult it is for him to get along without you, so he will miss you and appreciate what you do for him;

- a temporary absence can be used to try to motivate the batterer to seek help; your return is made conditional on his taking specific steps to get help and become less abusive;

- a temporary absence can give you a break — a period of temporary rest and relief from battering, even if you know it will continue when you go back;

- getting away for awhile can give you a chance to think more clearly (away from the everyday stresses and strains) about yourself, your relationship, and your future;

- a separation also provides time away from your partner's interference for you to make plans and

---

*The abusive partner can also learn to use this sort of temporary separation to control his behavior. When he realizes that he is becoming angry and liable to become physically assaultive, he takes a TIME-OUT. He leaves until he is able to calm down, in order to avoid a battering incident.

contacts that will help you become more independent;

- a temporary absence, whether it was meant to be temporary or not, is a way of testing yourself and gaining more experience being on your own away from your partner.

When you go back after a temporary separation, think about what you have accomplished. What effects did the separation have: on your partner, on your relationship with him, on you? Are things better now, the same, or worse? What did you learn as a result of the temporary separation? How "successful" it was depends, of course, on what you were trying to accomplish but it may also have brought some unexpected benefits. Chances are that a temporary separation, in itself, will not stop your partner from future battering, but you will not know that until you try it.

Practical Problems

For many battered women the problem is not so much a matter of mixed feelings and emotional ties to the batterer. At some point, they know they want to leave, but they are not sure how to go about it.

A battered woman's problems do not end when she decides to leave. Consider just a small part of what you must accomplish.

- Getting yourself and children safely out of the house.
- Finding a place to stay, short-term and long-term.
- Obtaining the money you need to live on your own.
- Raising your children as a single parent.

- Taking legal action.
- Resisting your partner's pleading and threats.

Leaving Safely

How difficult it will be to get safely away from the house depends on how violent the batterer is, how strongly he is opposed to your leaving, and how closely he watches you. Be very careful about this. When the time comes that you decide to leave, just go. For your own protection, be discreet in your preparations and *do not tell the batterer in advance.* Situations will come up in which you are tempted to tell him. For instance, you might be feeling insecure and unloved. You tell your husband or lover you are leaving as a "test" — of whether or not he still wants you enough to try to keep you from leaving. Look for another way to get the reassurance about yourself you need! Maybe instead you feel you owe your partner an explanation of what you are planning to do; "it's only fair." It is more important to be fair to yourself. Do not jeopardize your own safety at this critical time. Sometimes during an argument you might be tempted to tell your partner you are leaving to hurt him emotionally. This is dangerous because the more threatened and angry he feels, the more violent he may become. It is best not to threaten to walk out on him if he is already in a rage and there is no way for you, realistically, to get away from him just then. *Wait until you are someplace safe.* There will be plenty of time for explanations later.

Finding Shelter

Figure out in advance where you can stay for a day or two in an emergency. If you do not have a car you can use to get away or someone nearby who is able to drive you, call the police. Even if they do not arrest the batterer, the police can escort you and your children away from the house. Ask the police to take you to the nearest shelter for battered women, to the hospital, to a friend or relative's house, or even to the police station — whatever seems best depending on the circumstances. Especially if your partner is threatening to find you wherever you go and hurt you or the children or take you back by force, contact a shelter for battered women.

If your situation does not pose an immediate threat to your physical safety and you have more time to prepare for leaving, consider in advance what kind of housing might be available to you. Can friends or relatives take you in for a short time? Is there a shelter for battered women nearby? Is there any other emergency housing in your community? Could you share living quarters with someone else for an extended period of time and maybe share expenses until you can make it on your own? Go apartment hunting just to see what is available. How much do apartments cost per month? How much money is required as a security deposit. Are children welcome? Is there special low-income housing for which you might qualify? How do you apply? Is there a waiting list? Is there inexpensive student housing you could move into if you go back to school? Would it be better for you to move to another town or city? Do you have friends or relatives anywhere else with whom you could stay while you re-establish yourself in a new community? Check with the shelter for battered women nearest you to see if they can suggest a shelter to contact at your new location.

Sometimes Red Cross or other community-helping agencies can provide money for a bus ticket. Before leaving town, if you are worried about confrontation with the batterer, have the police escort you back to your old residence to pick up any personal belongings or documents you may have left behind.

Taking Legal Action

When you leave your partner, before making long-term plans, you should also consult a lawyer, if you have not done so earlier. Find out what the legal implications of a long-term separation will be. It is important to get good legal advice. Divorce laws vary from state to state. To apply for divorce in a particular state you have to meet its residency requirements. It might be to your advantage, though, to file for divorce in the county or state where you want to live if you are planning to move. You do not have to be divorced in the same state in which you were married.

Tell your lawyer about the battering. Be sure he or she understands the nature and extent of your spouse's abusive behavior. If you have children, discuss potential problems with custody, visitation, and support. Your partner's abusive behavior may extend to threats of what will happen to you if you try to divorce him: he will keep the house, car, or other material goods; he will cut you off financially; he will sue for custody of the children; he will show you up in court as an unfit wife and mother; etc. It is difficult not to panic sometimes in the face of this kind of browbeating. It is true that the outcome of a divorce action is never entirely certain at the start, but you can get an objective assessment from your lawyer. An attorney who knows the state laws and the inclinations of the courts in your particular area can help you sort out which threats have some basis in fact — and how best to address them — and which are unfounded. Get the support you need, professional and personal, so you can fight back against your spouse's attempts to intimidate you.

Financing Your New Life

For an extended separation from your partner you need a source of income. You can call the Department of Social Services and make an appointment to speak to a case-worker. Find out if you would qualify, if you separated from your partner, for Aid to Dependent Children, Food Stamps, or Medicaid programs. Ask, specifically, how much money you would receive for housing, food, utilities, phone, medical expenses, and so on. Ask whether there are any job training programs in which you can participate. Explore employment possibilities, including non-traditional jobs for women. Check the help-wanted ads in the newspaper. Ask around at different businesses in your area. Make an appointment to talk to a job counselor at the local branch of your State Employment Security Commission. Try to get some idea of the jobs available in your community and consider how the skills you have fit in.

If you want to go back to school, see an advisor at the school about financial aid. Loans or scholarships, combined with inexpensive student housing and flexible hours, may make it possible for you to manage higher education. Ask at the schools to which you are applying whether there are any special services for women with young children or older women who have been out of school for some time. If you are African-American, Native American, or Hispanic, ask about special programs for minority students. If you are not ready to try a four-year college program, talk to academic counselors at the junior college level about shorter, vocationally oriented courses of study. Look through their college catalog and see what attracts you. Consider your interests, your abilities, and your prospects in the job market. Community college fees are relatively inexpensive, and going back to school, even for a few credits at a time, could be just the thing to give you a new goal to work toward.

Final Note

Battered women who stay in abusive relationships often place great importance on the idea that they could not get along without their partner or that sometimes he is very good to them. Stop and think about it. Isn't being battered a high price to pay for the times in between that are still good? Each year women die as a result of assaults by a husband or lover. After years of abuse some women finally kill the man who batters them out of fear for their own lives or their children's safety. Once physical force enters a personal relationship, the effects can be deadly. The bottom line is that violence kills. It can result in serious physical injury, permanent disfigurement, or death. If not this time, next time. Meanwhile, the battering may be "killing" you emotionally. Without exaggerating the dangers, consider the very real risk you take living with a battering man as the cycle of violence repeats itself. If you tend to minimize the battering that goes on in your relationship by telling yourself it could be worse, do not forget that the next time it might be much worse.

Battered women who leave their partners give up whatever rewards or benefits they think there might be in staying because getting away from an abusive relationship comes to be more important to them. In spite of the difficulties ahead, leaving offers a battered woman the positive challenge of making changes in her own life. Setting new priorities beyond survival in the abusive relationship makes room for new hopes, new dreams, new directions. It means an opportunity to regain a sense of yourself and your own worth; greater freedom to decide what you want for yourself. If you are at a point right now where you are too bitter or too numb to think with any optimism about the future, consider that just the act of leaving, in itself, is an assertion of your right as a human being to be free of violence. Even if you have no idea where you are heading and are not ready to think about it yet, leaving is taking a positive step away from battering. To say that leaving is difficult does not mean you cannot do it! When you leave an abusive relationship, you free the time and thought and energy that went into trying to please your partner. You can use your time and thought and energy to make a new life for yourself instead. The strength, courage, endurance, and commitment that got you through the battering will help get you through the challenge of starting over, if you decide to leave. Remember, you are a survivor. You are more capable, and have more potential than you realize.

Deciding whether to stay or not to stay with a battering man is a very important and often difficult choice that no one else can make for you. However, this does not mean you have to do it all alone. Talk to other people — friends or relatives you trust, other battered women or staff members at a shelter for battered women, professional counselors. Listen and reflect on what you are saying about the relationship and your own feelings, values, and priorities as well as the advice given by others. Keep in mind that it is up to you to do what you think is best in your own particular situation. See Appendix C for a review and further suggestions.

10
Taking Stock, Taking Action

Woman battering came to be recognized as a social problem because a social movement arose which demanded that public attention be given to this condition. As a society, we were confronted with the gap between our ideal of family life and the reality of violence in the home. Many dedicated individuals worked long and hard to convince others that the problem of woman battering exists, and that it deserves attention. Individual and collective effort to educate the public and to provide support for victims of domestic assault are continuing. These efforts mean you are not alone. Many people do understand the nature of domestic assault and are active on your behalf.

Taking Stock

The idea of "taking stock," as used here, refers to making an appraisal of one's situation, linking individual experience to the larger social context in which it takes place. For you as a battered woman, taking stock means reflecting on your personal experience with an awareness that this experience is shaped by the way in which our society as a whole regards the issue of family violence. Seeing your private troubles against the background of woman battering as a larger social problem will help you understand why this has happened to you and what steps you can take to improve your situation. When you think about your individual circumstances, keep this overview in mind. Consider the following points:

- Woman battering is a widespread occurrence in our society. It is estimated that over 1.8 million women are severely battered each year. A woman is physically assaulted by a man with whom she lives in at least one out of 10 families.

- The shelter movement in the 1970's called attention to "wife beating." There are now over 1,000 programs for battered women throughout the United States. Woman battering is not only a private trouble, it is a recognized social problem.

- Battering is violent and abusive behavior directed toward one's partner in a personal relationship. Women are more likely than men to be victimized and have more difficulty leaving an abusive relationship. Victims of battering suffer physical and emotional harm.

- Woman battering happens when men learn to use force to establish control in intimate relationships. This takes place in a society that defines women as suitable targets and fails to intervene effectively to protect them.

- Society still tends to "blame the victim," but victims of battering do not cause themselves to be abused and they do not deserve to be beaten.

- Battering men often reject the idea that they have a problem with violence. They blame others for their actions. In order to change, battering men must take responsibility for their own behavior, realize that it is unacceptable, and work to change it.

- Few men, if any, quit battering on their own. The victim is left to deal with the problem of being in a relationship with an abusive partner. Battered women do have options and choices, but they need outside support.

- A battered women's resources include neighbors, family, friends, and acquaintances. Some will be more willing and better able to help than others in meeting the needs of a battered woman, but none should be overlooked as possible sources of help. Different people can help in different ways.

- Shelters for battered women offer a wide variety of essential services: safety from immediate physical harm, individual counseling and support groups, crisis-lines, information and referral, advocacy, community education, and more.

- Battered women need medical attention for their injuries. They may or may not wish to confide in their doctor about the source of the injuries, but should be cautious about using medication to cope with a battering relationship. Medical records help document the nature and extent of abuse.

- Professional counselors can be helpful to battered women, assisting them in sorting out the complex mix of feelings that being in an abusive relationship generates. The safety and well-being of the victim, not keeping the relationship together at all costs, must be the primary concern.

- Domestic assault is a crime. Batterers can be arrested and prosecuted. The legal system is complicated and not consistently responsive to the needs of battered women, but does provide one possible means for the individual and community to convey that woman battering is not acceptable.

- For many reasons, both practical and emotional, battered women do not find it easy to end a battering relationship. Deciding whether to stay or not to stay with their partner is a difficult choice, varying with each woman's individual circumstances. Leaving presents its own set of difficulties but also the possibility of a new start — a chance for the victim and her children to live without violence.

Taking Action

There is one important sense in which each battered woman is alone. You are a unique individual. No one else's life is exactly the same. Knowing that other women have also been battered does not change the facts of your own past experience. It does not erase the pain that you feel or the difficulties you face. There is no one right answer or solution for every woman who has been victimized by battering. Other people can help in many ways but in the end *it will be up to you to determine what you want from your life* and how to go about it. This kind of choice is often difficult. At times it may be more a matter of deciding what you do not want. Or, it may mean experimenting with different possibilities until you find a path that seems right for you.

In violent and abusive relationships, women often lose a sense of themselves. They lose a sense of competence and control over their lives. One of the consequences of battering is discouragement; being deprived of hope or spirit or confidence. You may find yourself slipping into a routine of "getting by" instead of "getting on" with your life. You may be giving up on yourself, feeling that you have no choice. Taking responsibility for yourself and for being an active agent of change in your life is crucial. The changes you decide to make do not have to be sudden or dramatic. Even the smallest step you take in a new direction, no matter what the immediate results, demonstrates your ability to direct your own action. If the results are not what you expected, you still have acquired new information to guide your next step. Change involves a process of trial and error; setting goals, trying to implement them, observing the results, re-evaluating the goals, and trying again.

After reflecting on your thoughts and feelings, and being as objective as you can be about the facts in your own particular case, *set some goals for yourself. Develop a plan of action.* What will you do to try to change your life for the better? Here is a review of some of the suggestions made in this book.

- Admit to yourself that you are being battered, and that without outside help the battering will continue.

- Plan ahead for an emergency.
- Talk to other people about the situation at home.
- Contact a shelter for battered women.
- Find out all you can about resources available in your community.
- Ask the battering man to go for counseling.
- Keep records.
- Sort out your feelings and options.
- Consider your long-term prospects.
- Prepare yourself to be more independent financially.
- Stay involved in activities and social relationships outside of home.
- Be good to yourself.
- See a doctor when you have been injured.
- File a complaint with the police or sheriff's department.
- See a lawyer.
- Get a restraining order.
- Follow through on criminal prosecution.
- Leave on a temporary basis if you are not ready for a permanent separation.
- Get a divorce.
- Move away.

Take the suggestions that seem most appropriate for you and make your own list. Add to the list other suggestions that you think you might want to follow. You can do this mentally or on paper. Each suggestion will serve as a goal you are setting for yourself. Pick one or two that seem the most urgent, needing immediate attention, and start there. Work on another one or two that seem the easiest, to build confidence. Decide what specific actions you can take to reach each goal, then take action! See what results you get. Evaluate how much closer you are to your goal after taking a specific action. If you are doing this in writing try organizing your notes as illustrated on page 109.

Remember that you do not control the results. Do not blame yourself if they are not what you wanted. You will already have succeeded in taking the action that seemed most reasonable to you at the time. Keep trying different strategies. Sometimes you will not yet be in a position to reach a particular goal. Get as close as you can for now, then take a break. Resolve to come back to it later. You can work on something else in the meantime.

Social Change

If you have been battered, another kind of action you might consider taking is social action — joining with others in the social movement to help battered women. Existing programs for battered women rely on volunteers to help. You do not have to be an "expert" to make a contribution. Volunteers are given training and are able to help with a wide variety of tasks. You may volunteer for answering phones, child care, transportation, maintenance and repairs, record keeping, fund raising, community talks, and so on. You can offer whatever time and ability you have to spare. Your main job is helping yourself, putting the pieces of your own life together. You may also be able to make a contribution by helping others.

If there is no program for battered women in your community you can help to start one. (For suggestions, see Appendix B, Part 2). It was women like yourself, women helping other women, who saw the need and opened the first shelters for women seeking refuge from domestic assault. As a battered woman you have a special role to play. You know firsthand the obstacles that keep women trapped in abusive relationships and the kinds of help battered women need. You know the effects that woman battering can have on its victims. You have a personal interest in bringing about social change — change in attitudes, in laws, in policies, in services available. You can help raise awareness in your community of the problem of woman battering and strengthen efforts to assist victims of domestic assault. Through your efforts, other battered women too may learn that they are not alone.

Plan of Action

Goals	Specific Actions Possible	Action Taken (✔)	Results	Conclusion
1. _____	a. _____	____		
	b. _____	____		
	c. _____	____		
	d. _____	____		
2. _____	a. _____	____		
	b. _____	____		
	c. _____	____		
	d. _____	____		
3. _____	a. _____	____		
	b. _____	____		
	c. _____	____		
	d. _____	____		
4. _____	a. _____	____		
	b. _____	____		
	c. _____	____		
	d. _____	____		
5. _____	a. _____	____		
	b. _____	____		
	c. _____	____		
	d. _____	____		

Appendix A
Three Battered Women

Case #1

A woman, 25, came in Sunday on the 5:30 a.m. bus with her three children. The two girls are three and six years old. The boy is four. Her husband has abused her since their wedding night, when he pushed her down some stairs. He has broken her collar bone, given her black eyes, and injured her back. He would not let her visit friends or go places with them. She had to be back from the store in a certain amount of time, or he would question and threaten her. He loosened the tires on her car but her brother used the car before she did and got into an accident. They have been separated for several months but he continues to harass her. During the last incident he forced her to have sex with him. Two weeks ago she overdosed herself with heart medication.

She has been to the shelter before. The couple started to go for counseling but after the second time he refused to go. He became regularly abusive, every two months or so. He would make a mess of the house then yell at her for not keeping it clean. His family also belittles her. He degrades her. He would ask the three-year-old girl, should I beat your mother today or just tie her up? He slapped one of the other children for watching cartoons because he wanted to watch something else. He swears at his wife, and says he does not care whether she comes back or not. He says he wants a divorce, but he keeps trying to get in touch with her.

When she told him she was going for counseling to a mental-health clinic, he told her she is a crazy lady and it was embarrassing to him that she needs that kind of help. The priest she went to earlier for help came to talk to her husband and she said she overheard the priest tell her husband that she eggs him on so she deserves to be hit. She wants to arrest her husband but is having trouble with the police and courts, even though he beat her at a friend's house, in front of a witness. The family has moved frequently because her husband could not hold a job. Last time he quit because he was not getting the raises he felt he deserved. She has not been able to find a job of her own.

The three-year-old daughter says she hates her mother and misses her father. The six-year-old is serious and aloof; at night she cries in her sleep. The social worker involved in this case believes that the girl may have been sexually molested by the father or by a 17-year-old boy who was visiting with the family. The four-year-old boy is angry and aggressive. He does not listen to anyone. He will walk up smiling then just start kicking and punching anyone in his way. He screams at mealtimes, swearing and punching his mother, not eating. He will not play with the other children at the shelter. He takes toys from other children, rips the toys apart, throws them, stomps on them. He cries when his mother is out of sight but does not cooperate with her when they are together. She tried to punish him by putting pepper in his mouth.

Case notes from a shelter worker

Case #2

A woman, 47, and two sons, 12 and 16 years old were escorted to the shelter by police at 12:30 a.m. on a Friday night. The mother and 12-year-old were crying hard. The older boy tried to comfort his mother between telling what had happened. Her husband got angry at her when she asked him to let her drive because he was swerving all over the road. He hit her several times in the car. When they got home he threw her around, tried to choke her, broke a table and a lamp. She fought back, striking him in the face. The 16-year-old son called the police. The father punched him too, yelling that he hates him, the boy is no son of his, etc. The 16-year-old hit his father and pinned him down until the police got there. The 12-year-old hid behind a chair. The younger son was upset and scared. He said he loves his Dad and wants to see him again but realizes they should move out. When not drinking the father buys them things. Now that they have left, the boys feel maybe this time their father will change.

This woman and her husband have been married 28 years. He is an alcoholic. They have all been to counseling. She still goes to Al-Anon. Nothing has helped him. He blames his problems on other people. She feels guilty. Her mother says she has ruined her own life. She is afraid of the hate and rage she feels toward him now. Together, she and her husband have a good income. She is a nurse; he is an insurance agent. Without both paychecks coming in she will not be able to give the children what they need. She says that maybe happiness and security are more important than the money. She is planning to leave town when the children finish school.

Case notes from a shelter worker

Case #3

Mary, 36, lived with a battering man. She met him at a time when she was emotionally vulnerable. Her husband had died after a long illness. She was dating a lot but finding herself still lonely and unhappy. She was looking for companionship and a sense that someone really cared for her. Ed made her feel special and loved. She wanted a relationship enough to overlook cues that he was not an ideal choice. He was jealous and dependent on her. "When he first hit me, I thought he didn't really mean it. I loved him, so I ignored it." The next few times he said he was sorry and promised it would never happen again. By this time Ed had moved in with her. She was trying to be a good partner to him and look after him.

When Ed got angry he would blame his abusive behavior on her failures and shortcomings. "According to him I couldn't do anything right. I provoked him." She knew he was under pressure at work and tried to do better. He did not like her smoking, so she quit. He did not like her friends, so she stopped seeing so much of them. "He didn't want me to have friends. The lady next door would come over to talk and he would say I was going with her." She did keep her job for a while. "People at work tried to get me to leave, but I felt I couldn't do it. With all the constant criticism at home I had started feeling that I just couldn't make it on my own. Who else would want me?"

Mary suppressed the hostility and resentment she began to feel, partly in fear of setting him off. By this time she knew she did not want to get married, but she generally questioned her own judgment. She was confused about how serious the violence was. "Maybe I am just imagining it is worse than it is. It's just a few cuts and bruises. He's not that dangerous." He was saying that he needed her and could not live without her, but at the same time had threatened to kill her. One violent episode started when he didn't like a meal she had cooked. He threw the food on the floor and grabbed her. "He had his hand over my mouth and was holding my nose. He started doing that to keep me from screaming, but he didn't know when to stop. Then I realized that whenever he wanted he could kill me . . . He had hit me and gone out for awhile. When he came back he just started all over again. This time he held a knife to my throat."

After this fight Mary left town to stay with a friend. "I was so shattered. I couldn't think of anything beyond saving my life. You can't think and plan until you feel safe . . . I needed help to start over again." In deciding to leave the relationship Mary had some positive self-images to draw on — competency in her earlier marriage, a good relationship with her mother, job skills, and experience. Mary and Ed did not have children together.

Their relationship had gone on for only two years. She was still fearful of him. After she left town he set the house where they had lived, which she owned, on fire. Mary had no money when she left but was able to stay at a shelter for battered women while she was looking for a new job. Now she is saving money to replace the front teeth Ed knocked out.

Case history reconstructed from interviews with women at a shelter

Appendix B
Suggested Readings

1. For readings that might be of use to you, check your local library or bookstores. (Request the assistance of a librarian or bookstore employee if you can't find something suitable on the shelves. Bookstores can do computer-assisted searches to help locate and order material for you.) Look for titles like the following:

Brinegar, Jerry L. *Breaking Free from Domestic Violence.* CompCare Publishers, 1992.

Bowker, Lee H. *Ending the Violence: A Guidebook Based on the Experiences of 1,000 Battered Women,* Rev. ed. Holmes Beach, Fla.: Learning Publications, 1998.

Buzawa, Eve S., and Carl G. Buzawa. *Domestic Violence: The Criminal Justice Responses.* Newbury Park, Calif.: Sage Publications, 1990.

Corry, Barbara, George Thomas, and Harriet Shapiro. *Understanding Domestic Violence: A Recovery Resource for Battered Women and Those Who Work with Them.* Care Program, 1993.

Domestic Violence, Stalking, Antistalking Legislation. Washington, D.C.: National Institute of Justice, Office of Justice Programs, 1996.

Fritz, Barbara, and Ron Kerner. *Domestic Violence & Its Effects on Children.* Bureau for At-Risk Youth, 1992.

Geffner, R., W.K. Cartwright, and K. Hartt. *Spouse-Partner Abuse: A Categorized Bibliography and Reference List.* Tyler, Tex.: Family Violence and Sexual Assault Institute, 1992.

Goelman, Deborah, and Roberta Valente. *When Will They Ever Learn: A Law School Report.* Chicago: Office for Victims of Crime, Office of Justice Program, U.S. Department of Justice, 1997.

Gondolf, Edward. *Men Who Batter: An Integrated Approach for Stopping Wife Abuse.* Holmes Beach, Fla.: Learning Publications, 1985.

Groetsch, Michael. *He Promised He'd Stop: Helping Women Find Safe Passage from Abusive Relationships*. Brookfield, Wis.: CPI Publishing, 1997.

Jones, Ann. *Next Time She'll Be Dead: Battering and How to Stop It*. Boston: Beacon Press Books, 1994.

Koss, Mary P. et al. *No Safe Haven: Male Violence Against Women at Home, at Work, and in the Community*. Washington, D.C.: American Psychological Association, 1994.

Kurland, Morton. *Coping with Family Violence*. New York: Rosen Publishing Group, 1990.

Marecek, Mary. *Breaking Free From Partner Abuse: Voices of Battered Women Caught in the Cycle of Domestic Violence*. Buena Park, Calif.: Morning Glory Press, 1993.

McGregor, Heather, and Andrew Hopkins. *Working for Change: The Movement Against Domestic Violence*. Concord, Mass.: Paul & Company Publishers, 1992.

McNulty, Faith. *The Burning Bed*. New York: Harcourt, Brace, Janovich, 1980.

NiCarthy, Ginny and Sue Davidson. *You Can Be Free: An Easy-to-Read Handbook for abused Women*. Seattle: The Seal Press, 1989.

Pagelow, Mildred. *Woman Battering*. Sage Publications, 1981.

Paymar, Michael. *Violent No More: Helping Men End Domestic Abuse*. Hunter House, 1992.

Reed, Robert D., and Danek S. Kaus. *Domestic Violence — Battered Women: How and Where to Find Facts and Get Help*. R & E Publishers, 1993.

Renzetti, Claire. *Violent Betrayal: Partner Abuse in Lesbian Relationships*. Thousand Oaks, Calif.: Safe, 1992.

Secretariat for Family, Laity, Women, and Youth Staff. *When I Call for Help*. A Pastoral Response to Domestic Violence Against Women. U.S. Catholic Conference, 1992.

Sipe, Beth, and Evelyn J. Hall. *I Am Not Your Victim: Anatomy of Domestic Violence.* Thousand Oaks, Calif.: Sage Publications, 1996.

Spence-Diehl, Emily. *Stalking: A Handbook for Victims.* Holmes Beach, Fla.: Learning Publications, 1999.

Stark, Evan. *Everything You Needed to Know About Family Violence.* New York: Rosen Publishing Group, 1993.

Sue, Myra, and Laurie Woods. *A Mediator's Guide to Domestic Abuse.* National Center on Women and Family Law, 1989.

2. Additional Resources

Spouse-Partner Abuse: A Categorized Bibliography and Reference List (1992) by R. Geffner, W.K. Cartwright, and K. Hartt can be ordered from the Family Violence and Sexual Assault Institute, 1310 Clinic Drive, Tyler, Texas 75701.

For a detailed and insightful account of woman battering and the shelter movement, see *Women and Male Violence: The Visions and Struggles of the Battered Women's Movement* by Susan Schechter, South End Press, Boston, 1982. The bibliography includes a list of manuals on various aspects of setting up and providing services for battered women.

To identify existing programs, refer to *Working on Wife Abuse* by Betsy Warrior. This is a comprehensive, regularly updated directory of programs for battered women available from Betsy Warrior, 46 Pleasant Street, Cambridge, MA 02139.

The Center for Women Policy Studies, 2000 P Street, N.W., Suite 508, Washington, DC 20036, (202) 872-1770, publishes a bimonthly newsletter, RESPONSE (To Family Violence and Sexual Assault), that provides information about battering. CWPS also has available a listing of programs nationwide for men who batter and will respond to telephone requests if you are seeking the name and address of the shelter or domestic-assault program nearest you.

If you are interested in starting a program for battered women in your own community, you can also contact the National Coalition Against Domestic Violence, 1728 N Street, N.W., Washington, DC 20036 for advice and referral to your state coalition or network.

Appendix C
Suggestions for Keeping Records

One of the recommendations made in Chapter 4 was to keep records. It is worth the effort of writing things down because such records will help to:

- determine what patterns there are, if any, in the abusive relationship;

- document the incidents of assault as a basis for legal action — civil or criminal;

- evaluate the effectiveness of your strategies for dealing with the violence.

The sample journal format presented in this appendix would be one way of keeping a monthly record that would show how things have been going from week to week. More detailed notes on specific battering incidents could also be kept. Examples are also provided of formats that might be useful for organizing information about resources that are available to you and keeping track of your contacts with outside agencies and assistance programs.

Sample Journal Format

Month of _____, 20___

	Week 1	Week 2	Week 3	Week 4
Monday:				
Tuesday:				
Wednesday:				
Thursday:				
Friday:				
Saturday:				
Sunday:				

Additional Notes:

Additional Notes:

Resources

Make a resource list of your own with the telephone numbers you might want to have at hand in an emergency. Here is a sample, with space to add names and addresses or other notes.

	Notes	**Phone**
Relatives		_____
		_____
		_____
Friends		_____
		_____
		_____
Neighbors		_____
		_____
		_____
Police	Emergency Calls	_____
		_____
Doctor		_____
Hospital		_____
Shelter for Battered Women	Crisis-line	_____
		_____
Lawyer		_____
		_____
Counseling		_____
		_____
Other:		_____
_____		_____
_____		_____
		_____
_____		_____

Contacts

Another kind of record you might want to keep is of the contacts you have made with people from outside agencies.

In your comments mention why you made this contact and how useful you felt the person was to you. This way you will be able to remember the names of the persons who have been most helpful so that you can contact them again. If you are referred to someone else, use the name of the person who referred you when you make your next contact.

Date	Name	Job Title

__ / __ / __   _____   _____

Comments:

Date	Name	Job Title

__ / __ / __   _____   _____

Comments:

Date	Name	Job Title

__ / __ / __   _____   _____

Comments:

Date	Name	Job Title

__ / __ / __   _____   _____

Comments:

Appendix D
Safety at Home*

➤ Make your home as safe as possible by changing the locks, adding dead bolts, and obtaining an apartment that is not on the first floor. Remove sharp objects and weapons from sight. Keep a telephone in a room that locks from the inside. If possible, purchase a cellular phone (or a special 911 phone) and keep it in a pocket or in an accessible hiding place; pre-program 911 (or the local police emergency number) or the number of a safe friend or relative into the phone's directory.

➤ Plan and practice an escape route out of the home and a safety plan for the children. Teach the children not to let the batterer in the home (unless the batterer has a legal right to be there). Prepare the children to respond to a batterer who comes to their school or day-care center; if a protection order includes provisions about the children, give a copy to the children's school or child-care facility.

➤ Keep a bag packed and hidden in a safe place at home (or locked in a car trunk with only one key), or with a safe relative or friend, in preparation for flight. It should include: money for phone calls, transportation, and one month's expenses, clothing, diapers, court documents, passports, identification (social security, driver's license, welfare identification, family photographs), birth certificates, school and medical records,

---

*Reprinted by permission of the American Bar Association from Deborah Goelman and Roberta Valente. *When Will They Ever Learn? Educating to End Domestic Violence: A Law School Report.* Chicago: Office for Victims of Crime, Office of Justice Programs, U.S. Department of Justice, 1997.

necessary medicines, credit cards, checkbooks, work permits, green cards, lease/mortgage payments, insurance papers, bank books, telephone/address books, car/house keys, and ownership documents for car/house.

➡ Make extra copies of protection orders and keep them in safe places. Attach a copy of the interstate protection order provisions of the Violence Against Women Act and proof of service to each protection order to minimize enforceability problems in other states. Show the orders to police officers to improve their response.

➡ Show neighbors a picture of the batterer and/or the batterer's vehicle so they can screen visitors and call the police if necessary. Batterers often gain access to apartment buildings by pretending to be someone else or by following tenants indoors.

Appendix E
Safety at Work*

➤ Give a picture of the batterer and the batterer's vehicle to security guards and colleagues at the workplace. If the batterer shows up, security or other workplace personnel can order the batterer to leave or call the police.

➤ Keep a copy of your protection order at work. Notify a supervisor or the Human Resources Department of the existence of the order and give them a copy.

➤ Screen calls with voice-mail or a machine if possible, or ask a colleague to screen calls or listen in on the line. Your lawyer may be able to introduce recorded threats made by the batterer as evidence in a court case.

➤ Travel with another person. Victims frequently are harassed on the way to or from work by batterers who are jealous of coworkers, or want victims to lose their jobs and become economically dependent on them.

*Reprinted by permission of the American Bar Association from Deborah Goelman and Roberta Valente. *When Will They Ever Learn? Educating to End Domestic Violence: A Law School Report.* Chicago: Office for Victims of Crime, Office of Justice Programs, U.S. Department of Justice, 1997.

Appendix F
Four Exercises for Sorting
Out Your Feelings and Options

Exercise 1 📄 Expressing Your Fears

My Fears

About Staying	About Leaving
_____	_____
_____	_____
_____	_____
_____	_____
_____	_____
_____	_____
_____	_____

Rather than avoiding them, try to get your fears out in the open by listing them, no matter how scary they feel or how silly you think they might seem to someone else. In no particular order, write down whatever fears come to mind when you think about staying in your present relationship. Now imagine you have decided not to stay, what feelings do you have then? What fears are connected with the idea of leaving? Putting your fears into words does not make them go away, but it does sometimes make them seem less overwhelming. It makes the fears easier to talk about and understand. It lets you begin to sort out different kinds of fears and examine what is behind them. Some are very specific (e.g., you are afraid of being injured by your partner the next time he gets angry); some are much more general (e.g., you are afraid of being alone). When a fear you have listed is very general, see if you can break it down. For example, what is it about the idea of being alone, specifically, that worries you? Compare the fears you have about staying with the fears about leaving. See what you are up against in each case. Try not to let your fears paralyze you. Fears are feelings, not behavior. You can act in spite of your fears, and you can act in ways that reduce your fears.

Exercise 2 📄 Identifying Rewards and Priorities

What I Get Out of Staying	What I Gain By Leaving
_____	_____
_____	_____
_____	_____
_____	_____
_____	_____
_____	_____
_____	_____

In this exercise try to list as completely as you can the rewards or benefits, large and small, you associate with staying and with leaving. A list like this should help clarify some of the reasons you have stayed with your partner. It identifies what you still get out of the relationship. Compare the benefits of staying and leaving. Is the list of what you gain by leaving very short? Does this mean that you actually have little to gain by leaving? Or, does it mean you have not thought as much about the benefits as about the difficulties involved? If you are discussing your situation with someone else, ask for their suggestions too. What do they think you might get out of staying or gain by leaving? If you are reading books about battering, see what the authors include as gains of leaving. How do you feel about these additions to your list?

Of all the items on each list, which are the most important to you? Circle or put a check next to the rewards you value most highly. The results will reflect the priorities you are setting for yourself at this time. For example, being free of your partner's abuse might be the thing you most value and want right now. Another kind of question to ask yourself in reviewing your answers in this exercise is whether it is possible for you to have some of the rewards and benefits you associate with staying if you decide, instead, to leave and vice versa. For example, what might you do in order to have more freedom and independence if you stay? In what different ways might you satisfy your desire for companionship if you leave? And so on down the two lists.

Exercise 3 📄 Examining Your Reasons for Not Leaving

I Can't or (Shouldn't)
Leave Because   **Counterarguments**

_____   _____
_____   _____
_____   _____
_____   _____
_____   _____
_____   _____

The purpose of this exercise is to let you critically examine some of the attitudes and assumptions that may be keeping you in a battering relationship. This decision may be based not so much on personal choice but rather on unquestioned beliefs that make it seem you have no choice. Here you first list all the reasons you believe you cannot or should not leave your partner. Then, when you have finished the first column, try to write down one or more arguments against each reason ("counterarguments"). Examples are given below.

Reasons for Not Leaving   **Counterarguments**

I shouldn't leave because it is wrong to break up the family. | It is my partner's violence that is breaking up our family; being abused is not my idea of being a family; a "broken" home is better for children than a violent home.

I can't leave because I love him.	If I stay I will hate him too; maybe this is the wrong kind of love if I cannot respect myself anymore; if he can love me and still beat me, I can love him and still leave him.
I shouldn't leave because he needs me; he has problems too.	He says he needs me, but not enough to stop battering me; he has to learn to deal with his problems, I can't solve them.
I can't leave because I have no way to support myself.	I could live for a while with my parents and look for a job, or try to go back to school; maybe I would not be as well off financially, but I would have more control over the money I did have; maybe I can't leave today, but I can start preparing to be able to support myself later.

The point of this exercise is not to convince you to leave. It is to get you to think about your options. Maybe when you sit down and question some of the reasons you have always thought you couldn't or shouldn't leave, you will not find them as convincing any more. You will realize that you really do not have to stay; you have a choice.

Exercise 4 📄 Appreciating Your Positive Qualities

My Strengths

_____

_____

_____

_____

_____

_____

_____

   List your strengths. What keeps you going? What are the good things about yourself? What do you like about yourself? What do others seem to like about you? Include all the positive qualities you can think of even if they do not seem very "big" or "important" to you right now. Think back to good qualities you had when you were younger and list them too, even if you think you have lost them. Include strengths you have demonstrated only at certain times or in certain situations; even a strength you showed only once. Add qualities you think you could develop — potential strengths. Finally, look over your list and consider what you have written in relation to the question of whether to stay or not to stay with the battering man. How will the qualities you have listed as your strengths work for you if you stay? How will the same qualities help you if you decide to leave? The most important part of this exercise is to get you to recognize your own strengths. Too often, battering leaves women feeling helpless and negative about themselves. Women, generally, are more often than men trained to be modest and self-effacing. This can become a serious handicap. Success and failure are partly a matter of your own perception. If I did this today, have I failed because I did not do more, or succeeded because I did this much? Why not think positively about what you have succeeded in doing? To face your fears and to make difficult decisions, it helps to appreciate your strengths and accomplishments.

The answers you come up with on all these exercises can serve as a starting point and guide for you, something to think about. The answers you give will probably change over time, so go back and re-examine these exercises from time to time. Make up some of your own. Go back to them whenever you want to take time out to sort through your feelings and options.

Appendix G
Steps in Pressing Charges and Sample Legal Forms

If you are a victim of woman battering you might wonder what is involved in pressing charges for domestic assault. The types of charges, the steps involved, and samples of forms typically used are included in this section.

Types of Charges

There are two kinds of criminal charges which might be brought against a battering man: misdemeanor and felony. Whether a particular action is a misdemeanor or a felony offense depends on how the laws in your state are written. How each type of offense is specifically defined — what it includes and what it does not — will vary with the criminal statutes from one state to another. Generally, though, a felony is a more serious offense with stricter legal penalties for conviction. For example, if your partner threatens you with a weapon or assaults you with intent to do great bodily harm he might be charged with a felony. The misdemeanor is a less serious charge with less severe penalties for conviction. Assault and battery, for example, is a misdemeanor which typically refers to use of physical force against another person when little or no physical damage occurs to the person as a result. When injuries sustained are more serious and require medical treatment, the misdemeanor charge of Aggravated Assault might be appropriate. Except in extreme cases domestic assault tends to be treated by the legal system as a misdemeanor.

Steps Involved

Step 1 — The Police / Sheriff's Report

The first step is to file a complaint with the police department or sheriff's department. A report will then go from the police or sheriff's department to the prosecuting attorney's office for screening.

File a complaint as soon after a battering incident as possible. If police or other law enforcement officers are called to your home, tell them what happened in as much detail as you can. Point out to the officers who are present the physical signs of injury to yourself and any other damage done by your partner. Tell them if your partner has been abusive at other times and whether there were any witnesses to this assault. Ask that all this information be included in their report. If law enforcement officers are not called to the scene of the assault or if you are afraid to make an official complaint at the time of the assault because your partner is present, you may still file a complaint later by going to the police or sheriff's department and reporting what happened. Be specific about what your partner did and about the injuries that resulted. If you are hospitalized, you can request that an investigating officer be sent to take a complaint from you. It is best not to wait more than òne or two weeks to make a report if you think you might want to press charges.

Step 2 — The Prosecuting Attorney's Office

After a report is received from the police or sheriff's department by the prosecuting attorney's office you will be interviewed by an assistant prosecuting attorney to determine whether the complaint will be authorized for prosecution. If the assistant prosecuting attorney reviewing your case believes there is a reasonable possibility of conviction, the complaint will be authorized; otherwise it will be denied.

The prosecutor's office will be concerned with the events that took place as they relate to criminal statutes (laws) that have been violated, evidence available to support the complaint if it is brought to court, and your willingness to cooperate in pursuing the case. If your complaint is not accepted for prosecution, you may be able to appeal this decision. Request a second opinion from the prosecuting attorney's office. Whichever way the decision goes, ask for an explanation. Get as much information as you can about the basis on which the decision to deny or to follow through on your complaint is being made. Even if you are not able to have your assailant prosecuted this time, you will have a better idea of what to do next time if you are still interested in pressing charges. When a case is accepted for prosecution it may be passed on from one assistant attorney to the next so that you have to deal with a different person at each step. Ask that your case be permanently assigned to one individual if there is someone available with whom you feel especially well-represented.

Step 3 — The Judge

After your complaint is authorized by the prosecuting attorney's office you will be asked to sign the complaint in the presence of a judge.

Someone from the prosecuting attorney's office may accompany you or you may simply be asked to go to another building where the court with jurisdiction in your case is located. A sample copy of a misdemeanor complaint, presenting the nature of the assault and the specific laws which the prosecutor's office believes to have been violated, is presented later in this appendix. Though the form used will not be identical in every community, this sample represents the kind of form which will be signed by you (the "complaining witness") and the judge. Note that the sample form is stamped "DOMESTIC VIOLENCE." In response to growing awareness of the unique nature of cases of domestic violence as compared to other types of assault (and corresponding changes in legislation in some states), this complaint has been clearly identified as involving domestic assault. If this procedure is not followed in your own community, ask what special attention, if any, is given to domestic violence cases.

Step 3 — Action on Warrant

The complaint signed by a judge become the basis for the court to issue a warrant for the assailant's arrest. A warrant is a legal document authorizing the police or other law enforcement officers to arrest the offender ("Defendant") and bring him before the court. The warrant is sent by the court to the police or sheriff's department for action.

If your assailant is not already in custody (having been taken to jail earlier, when the assault took place), the police will not seek him out on a misdemeanor charge. He will be notified by mail that he must come in and appear in court. If the charge is a felony, when a warrant is received by the police or sheriff's department, officers will be sent out to arrest him. You should be aware that there is a great deal of variation in how vigorously individual law enforcement agencies will pursue the arrest.

Step 5 — The Arraignment

Arraignment is the step in which the person accused of a crime comes before a judge and the charges against him are presented to him. He will then enter his plea, "guilty" or "not guilty." This means that he admits to the actions cited in your complaint or he denies those actions.

Neither you nor a prosecuting attorney will be present at this time, although the defendant may have an attorney present with him. It is still important for you to keep informed about when the arraignment will take place. If the defendant (your battering partner) pleads guilty, the court may sentence him at that time. The prosecuting attorney's office will not always be informed about the time of arraignment, so check with the police or the court to find out when the defendant in your case is scheduled for arraignment.

Step 6 — The Pre-sentence Conference

Before the judge sentences a defendant who pleads guilty at time of arraignment the judge may order a preliminary investigation or pre-sentence conference to obtain additional information that will be helpful in determining an appropriate sentence.

What you have to say about past abuse, the extent of injury done, the likelihood of future assault, and your own preferences with respect to the sentence given should be heard at this time. This is not to say that your wishes will be followed precisely but they will be taken into consideration. Your input is important in providing the judge with a more detailed picture of the circumstances involved. Otherwise the judge may sentence without being fully aware of a pattern of battering that goes beyond this one assault or how the batterer's sentence will affect you.

If the court has its probation staff prepare a pre-sentence report you can call the probation department and ask to have a statement from you included. Address your statement to the judge and identify the defendant (your batterer) by name at the start. Describe the basic pattern of abuse you have experienced from the defendant and its effects on you and on your children. Refer to your medical records if you sought treatment for injuries. Attach copies of letters or notes from your partner in which he admitted to having been abusive. If you are seeking a divorce or legal separation include that information. If you have had to relocate to avoid him, or if your life has been disrupted in other ways by his abuse, say so in your statement. Also, if your batterer has a past criminal record, ask the probation officer you are working with to check on his prior convictions. Then be sure this information is passed on to the court.

Step 7 — The Pre-trial Conference

If the defendant pleads not guilty at his arraignment, a pre-trial conference will probably be held, about 10 days to one month after the arraignment. At a pre-trial conference the prosecuting attorney meets and talks with the defendant and his lawyer. The defendant is shown the police report on his case. The defendant can ask for a jury trial or a bench trial, or change his plea to guilty. If the prosecutor's office agrees, he may plead guilty to a lesser offense (e.g., Assault and Battery rather than Aggravated Assault) to avoid going to trial. Depending on the procedures followed in your own community you may or may not need to be present at a pre-trial conference. One reason you might want to arrange to be there is that if your assailant changes his plea to guilty sentencing can follow.

Step 8 — The Trial

If there is a trial it may not take place for six weeks to one year later. Usually a trial will take place within about two months. A bench trial (before a judge without a jury) will generally occur sooner than a jury trial. You may receive a subpoena from the court. The subpoena is an official document which informs you that you are required to appear in court. You will be asked to testify concerning the facts of the particular assault for which your partner is being tried. Accounts of past abuse may or may not be admissible as evidence during the trial. Discuss this with the prosecuting attorney handling your case. Witnesses may be called to testify and other evidence like police reports and medical records may be introduced to support your case. You can expect the lawyer defending your partner to try to discredit your testimony. It may help to practice answering difficult questions beforehand. Try to get an idea what kinds of questions and issues may come up in court and have a friend, relative, counselor, or advocate rehearse them with you, as if you were at the trial. If you have never seen an actual trial and would like to sit in on one, check with your local court clerk to find out when one is scheduled that you could attend.

If your partner is found not guilty, he is free to go. If he is found guilty he will probably be released until sentencing, which should occur within a month. Here again, you might want to have a say if there is a pre-sentence investigation (especially if, for some reason, evidence of past abuse was not allowed to be presented at the trial).

Sentencing

If your assailant is convicted of a misdemeanor domestic assault any one or a combination of the following penalties might apply:

- Fines   About $100-$500 plus court costs.

- Jail   Not routine for first conviction on a misdemeanor offense but could be up to 90 days or one year; likelihood of a jail sentence goes up as the severity of injury caused increases, if the charge is a felony, and if the offender has a record of prior convictions for assault.

- Probation   Establishes terms (with which the offender must comply or face the possibility of time in jail), such as: report once a month to a probation officer; no contact with spouse; restitution to victim; and/or mandatory counseling. The threat of a jail sentence for violation of the terms of probation gives the court leverage in attempting to change the offender's behavior.

Sample Warning Letter

Office of the
PROSECUTING ATTORNEY
County of _____

James T. Smith – Prosecuting Attorney

                                                     January 10, 2000

Mr. John Doe
600 Avenue
Kalamazoo, MI 49001

Dear Mr. Doe:

  Please be advised that a criminal complaint has been filed with the Kalamazoo Police Department alleging that you committed an Assault and Battery upon one Jane Doe. The matter has been investigated and presented to this Office for the filing of criminal charges against you.

  I have reviewed the case and believe there exists adequate evidence to charge the crime of Assault and Battery. However, Mrs. Doe has requested that this letter be sent in lieu of criminal prosecution. It is her hope and mine that this warning letter will serve to prevent you from engaging in similar conduct in the future.

  I trust this warning has and will serve its intended purpose. It you have any questions regarding this matter, please contact me.

Very truly yours,

_____
  Assistant Prosecuting Attorney

SAMPLE COMPLAINT FORM

STATE OF MICHIGAN 9-1 JUDICIAL DISTRICT COURT ORI	**COMPLAINT** MISDEMEANOR	CASE NO.
Court address		Court telephone no.

THE PEOPLE OF ☒ THE STATE OF MICHIGAN ☐ _____ Vs. JOHN DOE DOB: Defendant Charge Witnesses	OFFENSE INFORMATION	
	Date on or about 10/23/	Police agency KPD
	City/Twp./Village and County in Michigan City of Kalamazoo County of Kalamazoo	
	Victim or Complainant JANE DOE	
	Complaining witness same	

STATE OF MICHIGAN, COUNTY OF   KALAMAZOO

The complaining witness says that on the date and at the location stated above, the Defendant(s), contrary to law,
did make an assault, or an assault and battery upon the following person: JANE DOE;
contrary to § 750.81, CL 1970; MSA § 28.276.   [750.81]

MISDEMEANOR: 90 days and/or $100.00.

ASSAULT OR ASSAULT AND BATTERY

DOMESTIC VIOLENCE

The complaining witness asks that Defendant(s) be apprehended and dealt with according to law.

X
Complaining witness signature

Warrant authorized on   10-24-
                        Date   by:
X
Prosecuting official
	Subscribed and sworn to before me on _____
	                                                    Date
	X
	District Judge/Court Clerk/Magistrate signature

COMPLAINT, MISDEMEANOR

COURT COMPLAINT FORMAT

SAMPLE WARRANT

STATE OF MICHIGAN 9–1 JUDICIAL DISTRICT	**WARRANT** MISDEMEANOR	CASE NO.
COURT ORI		
Court address		Court telephone no.

THE PEOPLE OF ☒ THE STATE OF MICHIGAN ☐ _____	OFFENSE INFORMATION	
Vs.	Date on or about 10/23/	Police agency KPD
JOHN DOE	City/Twp./Village and County in Michigan City of Kalamazoo County of Kalamazoo	
DOB Defendant	Victim or Complainant JANE DOE	
Charge	Complaining witness same	
Witnesses		

STATE OF MICHIGAN, COUNTY OF ___KALAMAZOO___

To any Peace Officer or Court Officer authorized to make an arrest: The complaining witness has filed a sworn complaint in this court stating that on the date and the location stated above, the Defendant(s), contrary to law,

did make an assault, or an assault and battery upon the following person: JANE DOE; contrary to § 750.81, CL 1970; MSA § 28.276.   [750.81]

MISDEMEANOR: 90 days and/or $100.

ASSAULT OR ASSAULT AND BATTERY

DOMESTIC VIOLENCE

F I L E D — 1 NOV
9TH DISTRICT COURT

Upon examination of the complaint, I find probable cause to believe Defendant committed the offense set forth. THEREFORE, IN THE NAME OF THE PEOPLE OF THE STATE OF MICHIGAN, I command you to arrest and bring Defendant before the court immediately, or the Defendant may be released when a cash or surety bond is posted in the amount of $ _____ for personal appearance before the court.

___11/4/___	(SEAL)	X _____
Date		District Judge/Magistrate

By virtue of this warrant the Defendant has been taken into custody as commanded.

___11/13/___		X _____
Date		Peace Officer

WARRANT MISDEMEANOR   **COURT WARRANT**

SAMPLE A-PRELIMINARY INJUNCTION

PRELIMINARY INJUNCTIVE ORDER—Divorce.   **6314**

State of Michigan,

Circuit Court for the County of ...... Kalamazoo ....

.... JANE DOE ....
                                        PLAINTIFF.   PRELIMINARY
                                                                          INJUNCTIVE ORDER
vs.

.... JOHN DOE ....   File No. ....
                                        DEFENDANT.

At a session of the above-entitled Court held in the Court House at ... Kalamazoo ....,

Michigan, on ...., 19...... ;

            Present: HONORABLE ...., Circuit Judge.

On the reading and filing the ...... Complaint .... of ... Plaintiff ....,

.... Jane Doe .... praying for a preliminary injunction and the Court

being fully advised, and,

            It appearing that .... Jane Doe .... will suffer

the following:[1] possible great bodily harm and loss of her life as threatened by the

Defendant, he having beaten her on more than one occasion ....,

unless a preliminary injunction order be issued; that said injury is irreparable because should the

threatened great bodily harm and/or loss of her life become a reality, it would

be irreparable. ....

            It Is Ordered that .... John Doe ...., his

agents, servants, employees and attorneys and those in active concert or participation with him who receive

actual notice of this order do absolutely desist and refrain from threatening, abusing, striking,
harrassing, assaulting, beating, molesting or wounding Plaintiff in any way
and in addition thereto he be, and is hereby, restrained from coming to the
Plaintiff's place of residence, it not being the marital home of the parties, at
(SPECIFIC ADDRESS IS GIVEN HERE), or any other place whatsoever, except for the
sole and only purpose, with the express permission of said Plaintiff, of visitation
of the minor children of the parties pursuant to the provisions of MSA 28,874.
            IT IS FURTHER ORDERED that a certified copy of this Order and proof of service
of said Order on the Defendant, JOHN DOE, shall be filed with (NAME OF SPECIFIC..,
POLICE AGENCY WITH JURISDICTION OVER PLAINTIFF'S ADDRESS IS GIVEN HERE.)
            It Is Further Ordered that bond in the amount of ....

...........................($.............) be given by ....

before said preliminary injunction be issued. [2] ....

....

....

....

Issued ...., 19......, at .... o'clock in the .... noon.

                                    X ....
                                            Circuit Judge.

1. Specify what immediate and irreparable injury, loss or damage or physical injury the petitioner will suffer.
2. If security is not required state reason why security is unnecessary.

Appendix H
Safety in Court*

➤ Arrive in court after your lawyer so that you are not alone with the batterer. If this is impossible, wait near a security guard or a bailiff. Be aware that batterers often physically assault, repeatedly harass, or emotionally coerce victims in court.

➤ Sit at a physical distance from the batter talk to your lawyer or wait for the case to be called. Always position your lawyer between you and the batterer. Batterers control and threaten their former victims simply by using body language.

➤ Do not speak to the batterer. Even if your layer is present, he may be unaware that the batterer is threatening you. Have your lawyer discuss any settlement negotiations with the batterer (or the batterer's lawyer if represented by counsel) and then report back to you.

➤ Take the same precautions with the batterer's family members. In domestic violence cases, it is not uncommon for the batterer's family members to physically assault or verbally abuse the victim in court. Safeguard children if the batterer or family members insist on holding them.

➤ Make certain that you are safe when exiting the courthouse. Batterers often stalk victims to discover where they live, or to punish victims for taking legal action.

---

*Reprinted with permission from the American Bar Association from Deborah Goelman and Roberta Valente, *When Will They Ever Learn? Educating to End Domestic Violence: A Law School Report.* Chicago: Office for Victims of Crime, Office of Justice Programs, U.S. Department of Justice, 1997.

Appendix I
State Resources*

State Coalitions on Domestic Violence

The following coalitions may be contacted for information about local batterer interventions, shelters, and community coalitions concerned with domestic violence, In addition, many coalitions are involved with the development of batterer intervention standards or guidelines in their states.

Alabama Coalition Against Domestic Violence
P.O. Box 4762
Montgomery, AL 36101
(334) 832-4842
(334) 832-4803 (fax)

Alaska Network on Domestic Violence
and Sexual Assault
130 Seward Street, Room 501
Juneau, AK 99801
(907) 596-3650
(907) 463-4493 (fax)

Arizona Coalition Against Domestic Violence
100 West Camelback Street, Suite 109
Phoenix, AZ 95013
(602) 279-2900
(602) 279-2980 (fax)

Arkansas Coalition Against Domestic Violence
#1 Sheriff Lane, Suite C
Little Rock, AR 72114
(501) 812-0571
(501) 371-0450 (fax)

*Reprinted with permission from the publisher from *Batterer Intervention: Program Approaches and Criminal Justice Strategies*. Washington, D.C.: National Institute of Justice, U.S. Department of Justice, 1998.

California Alliance Against Domestic Violence
619 Thirteenth Street, Suite I
Modesto, CA 95354
(209) 524-1888
(209) 524-0616 (fax)

Colorado Domestic Violence Coalition
P.O. Box 18902
Denver, CO 80218
(303) 831-9632
(303) 832-7067 (fax)

Connecticut Coalition Against Domestic Violence
135 Broad Street
Hartford, CT 06105
(860) 524-5890
(860) 249-1408 (fax)

D.C. Coalition Against Domestic Violence
P.O. Box 76069
Washington, DC 20013
(202) 783-5332
(202) 387-5684 (fax)

Delaware Coalition Against Domestic Violence
P.O. Box 847
Wilmington, DE 19899
(302) 658-2958
(302) 658-5049 (fax)

Florida Coalition Against Domestic Violence
1535 C-5 Killearn Center Boulevard
Tallahassee, FL 32308
(800) 500-1119
(904) 668-6862
(904) 668-0364 (fax)

Georgia Advocates for Battered Women and Children
250 Georgia Avenue, S.E., Suite 308
Atlanta, GA 30312 (900) 643-1212
(404) 524-3847
(404) 524-5959 (fax)

Hawaii State Coalition Against Domestic Violence
98-939 Moarialua Road
Aiea, HI 96701-5012
(808) 486-5072
(808) 486-5169 (fax)

Iowa Coalition Against Domestic Violence
1540 High Street, Suite 100
Des Moines, IA 50309-3123
(800) 942-0333
(515) 244-8028
(515) 244 7417 (fax)

Idaho Coalition Against Sexual and Domestic Violence
200 North Fourth Street, Suite 10-K
Boise, ID 83702
(208) 384-0419
(208) 331-0687 (fax)

Illinois Coalition Against Domestic Violence
730 Last Vine Street, Suite 109
Springfield, IL 62703
(217) 789-2830
(217) 799-1939 (fax)

Indiana Coalition Against Domestic Violence
2511 East 46th Street, Suite N-3
Indianapolis, IN 46205
(800) 332-7385
(317) 543-3908
(317) 568-4045 (fax)

Kansas Coalition Against Sexual and Domestic Violence
820 S.E. Quincy, Suite 416
Topeka, KS 66612
(913) 232-9784
(913) 232-9937 (fax)

Kentucky Domestic Violence Association
P.O. Box 356
Frankfort, KY 40602
(502) 875-4132
(502) 875-4268 (fax)

Louisiana Coalition Against Domestic Violence
P.O. Box 3053
Hammond, LA 70404-3053
(504) 542-4446
(504) 542-6561 (fax)

Maine Coalition for Family Crisis Services
128 Main Street
Bangor, ME 04401
(207) 941-1194
(207) 941-2327 (fax)

Maryland Network Against Domestic Violence
11501 Georgia Avenue, Suite 403
Silver Spring, MD 20902-1955
(800) MD-HELPS
(301) 942-0900
(301) 929-2589 (fax)

Massachusetts Coalition of Battered Women's Service Groups/Jane Doe Safety Fund
14 Beacon Street, Suite 507
Boston, MA 02108
(617) 248-0922
(617) 248-0902 (fax)

Michigan Coalition Against Domestic Violence
P.O. Box 16009
Lansing, MI 48901
(517) 484-2924
(517) 372-0024 (fax)

Minnesota Coalition for Battered Women
450 North Syndicate Street, Suite 122
St. Paul, MN 55104
(800) 646-0994 (in 612 Area Code)
(573) 646-6177
(573) 646-1527 (fax)

Missouri Coalition Against Domestic Violence
331 Madison Street
Jefferson City, MO 65101
(314) 634-4161
(314) 636-3728 (fax)

Mississippi State Coalition Against Domestic Violence
P.O. Box 4703
Jackson, MS 39296-4703
(800) 998-3234
(601) 981-9196
(601) 982-7372 (fax)

Montana Coalition Against Domestic Violence
P.O. Box 633
Helena, MT 59624
(406) 443-7794
(406) 449-9193 (fax)

Nebraska Domestic Violence and
Sexual Assault Coalition
315 South Ninth #18
Lincoln, NE 68508-2253
(800) 876-6238
(402) 476-6256

Nevada Network Against Domestic Violence
2100 Capurro Way, Suite E
Sparks, NV 89431
(800) 500-1556
(702) 358-1171
(702) 358-0546 (fax)

**New Hampshire Coalition Against
Domestic and Sexual Violence**
P.O. Box 353
Concord, NH 03302-0353
(800) 852-3388
(603) 224-8893
(603) 228-6096 (fax)

New Jersey Coalition for Battered Women
2620 Whitehorse/Hamilton Square Road
Trenton, NJ 08690
For Battered Lesbians: (800) 224-021 1 (in NJ only)
(609) 584-8107
(609) 584-9750 (fax)

New Mexico State Coalition Against Domestic Violence
P.O. Box 25363
Albuquerque, NM 87125
(800) 773-3645 (in NM only)
(505) 246-9240
(505) 246-9434 (fax)

New York State Coalition Against Domestic Violence
79 Central Avenue
Albany, NY 12206
(900) 942-6906
(518) 432-4864
(518) 432-4864 (fax)

North Carolina Coalition Against Domestic Violence
P.O. Box 51875
Durham, NC 27717
(919) 956-9124
(919) 682-1449 (fax)

North Dakota Council on Abused Women's Services
State Networking Office
418 East Rosser Avenue, Suite 320
Bismarck, ND 58501
(800) 472-2911 (in ND only)
(701) 255-6240
(701) 255-1904 (fax)

Ohio Domestic Violence Network
4041 North High Street, Suite 101
Columbus, OH 43214
(800) 934-9840
(614) 784-0023
(614) 784-0033 (fax)

Oklahoma Coalition Against Domestic
Violence and Sexual Assault
2200 North Classen Blvd, Suite 610
Oklahoma City, OK 73801
(800) 522-9054
(405) 557-1210
(405) 557-1296 (fax)

Oregon Coalition Against Domestic and Sexual Violence
520 Northwest Davis Street, Suite 310
Portland, OR 97204
(503) 223-7411
(503) 223-7490 (fax)

Pennsylvania Coalition Against Domestic Violence/
National Resource Center on Domestic Violence
6440 Flank Drive, Suite 1300
Harrisburg, PA 17112-2778
(800) 932-4632
(717) 545-6400
(717) 545-9456 (fax)

Rhode Island Coalition Against Domestic Violence
422 Post Road, Suite 104
Warwick, RI 02888
(800) 494-8100
(401) 467-9940
(401) 467-9943 (fax)

South Carolina Coalition Against
Domestic Violence and Sexual Assault
P.O. Box 7776
Columbia, SC 29202-7776
(800) 260-9293
(803) 750-1222
(803) 750-1246 (fax)

South Dakota Coalition Against
Domestic Violence and Sexual Assault
P.O. Box 141
Pierre, SD 57401
(800) 572-9196
(605) 945-0969
(605) 945-0870 (fax)

Tennessee Task Force Against Domestic Violence
P.O. Box 120972
Nashville, TN 37212
(800) 356-6767
(615) 386-9406
(615) 383-2967 (fax)

Texas Council on Family Violence
8701 North Mopac Expressway, Suite 450
Austin, TX 78759
(512) 794-1133
(512) 794-1199 (fax)

Domestic Violence Advisory Council (Utah)
120 North 200 West
Salt Lake City, UT 84145
(800) 897-LINK
(801) 538-4100
(801) 539-3993 (fax)

Vermont Network Against
Domestic Violence and Sexual Assault
P.O. Box 405
Montpelier, VT 05601
(802) 223-1302
(802) 223-6943 (fax)

Virginians Against Domestic Violence
2850 Sandy Bay Road, Suite 101
Williamsburg, VA 23185
(800) 838-VADV
(804) 221-0990
(804) 229-1553 (fix)

Washington State Coalition Against Domestic Violence
2101 Fourth Avenue East, Suite 103
Olympia, WA 98506
(800) 562-6025
(360) 352-4029
(360) 352-4078 (fax)

West Virginia Coalition Against Domestic Violence
P.O. Box 85
181B Main Street
Sutton, NW 26601-0085
(304) 765-2250
(304) 765-5071 (fax)

Wisconsin Coalition Against Domestic Violence
1400 East Washington Avenue, Suite 232
Madison, WI 53703
(608) 255-0539
(608) 255-3560 (fax)

Wyoming Coalition Against Domestic
Violence and Sexual Assault
341 East E. Street, Suite 135A
Pinedale, WY 82601
(800) 990-3877
(307) 367-4296
(307) 235-4796 (fax)

Appendix J
National Sources of Help

Health Resource Center on Domestic Violence
Family Violence Prevention Fund
383 Rhode Island Street, Suite 304
San Francisco, CA 94103-5133
(800) 313-1310
(415) 252-8991 (fax)

Provides information packets for health-care response to domestic violence.

Resource Center on Child Custody and Child Protection
National Center for Juvenile and Family Court Judges
P.O. Box 8970
Reno, NV 89507
(800) 527-3223
(702) 784-6160 (fax)

Provides information within the context of domestic violence.

National Domestic Violence Hotline
(800) 799-SAFE
(800) 787-3224

Provides information on local shelters and domestic violence programs.